Airbnb Investing

and Hosting

How to Start Your Airbnb Business Off Right:
Being a Superhost, Planning Your Taxes &
How to Make Money on Airbnb for a Passive
Income and Flexible Lifestyle

Mike Hartley

Mike Hartley

Disclaimer Notice:

The presented work is strictly informational and should not be interpreted as an offer to buy or sell any form of security, instrument, or investment vehicle. Furthermore, the information contained herein should not be taken as a legal, tax, accounting or investment recommendation given by the author(s) or any affiliated company, employees, or paid contributors. In other words, the information is presented without considering individual preferences for specific investments in terms of risk parameters. It is general information that does not account for a person's lifestyle and financial objectives. It is important to note that no tailored advice will be provided based on the given information.

The authors and their parent company, along with all employees and paid contributors, have agreed to abstain from trading any stock or investment written about for at least two days publication of any new article, book, report, or email. This includes any equity, options, debt, or other instruments related to that security, stock, or company, except for existing orders that pre-existed the submission; all such charges will be disclosed inside the document. The author(s) may have direct or indirect positions in some of the companies mentioned because of holdings in mutual funds, exchange-traded funds, closed-end funds, or other similar vehicles. Such indirect holdings are usually not disclosed as there is no guarantee that the author(s) is aware at any given time of the individual portfolios of any of these funds. Furthermore, certain decisions by these funds, such as buying or selling stocks, could potentially impact an author's position even if it was not done directly by them.

Warning:

There is no simple, easy way to become wealthy, especially regarding investments in the financial markets. While it may be possible to make a significant return on your investment, there is also a high risk of losing a large amount of money if you do not have the proper knowledge and knowledge base. You must conduct thorough research and analysis to succeed with investments with the most significant potential for price appreciation. Investing wisely requires an extensive level of education and an understanding of how markets work for one's portfolio to yield positive returns over time. Before venturing into any investment endeavor, it is essential to consult an experienced financial advisor or professional who can advise what steps should be taken and how much capital should be invested. It is also necessary to review all relevant information about potential investments, such as the company's financial statements and prospectus, to make an informed decision regarding whether to invest. Everyone must remember that past results are not necessarily indicative of future performance, so it is wise never to invest more money than you can afford to lose.

This work is based upon a thorough analysis of SEC filings, current news events, interviews, corporate press releases, and knowledge obtained through our experience as financial traders, investors, journalists, and educators. We encourage readers to be careful when making decisions involving their finances, as they are ultimately responsible for the outcomes of their choices. To ensure they have thoroughly informed themselves before making any investment decisions, we strongly advise readers to take the time to research each subject in more detail by seeking out additional sources such as third-party analysts or other reading materials on the web. Furthermore, we recommend conducting a comprehensive review of all available data to ensure each conclusion is well-rounded and sound by exploring multiple aspects of an issue or topic. Ultimately, we believe that a person's financial future will benefit from making prudent and informed decisions based on knowledge gathered from various sources.

Foreword to the Series

Investing is a necessary and invaluable life skill that many people don't even realize they need. It allows you to create financial stability, accomplish your most ambitious goals, and secure your future. Whether it be providing for loved ones, avoiding the need to work past retirement age, or funding a dream vacation in Japan, investing requires a deep understanding of the principles of finance as well as those of self-discipline, patience, and sound judgement, free from any emotion or prejudice. While this may feel intimidating at first glance, investing can be extremely manageable with the right guidance and strategies that minimize risks while maximizing returns. By staying informed and educated on the basics of investing, we'll have you on the road to financial success.

Whilst this series masquerades as a comprehensive set of educational guides to the various inroads of investing, it is in fact a chronology of what I have learnt over the years - and from almost every aspect of investing there is. Growing up in a family that had relatively few financial resources, I was always driven to make something of myself and ensure the future security of my loved ones. One of the ways I set out to do this was by ambitiously aiming to make a million dollars in cold hard cash - which seems almost comical when I look back on it now as I had no idea why I chose this figure! A million dollars was just an arbitrary number that I decided upon when I didn't fully comprehend what it meant, or how life-changing it could be. I just thought to myself "I think having a sum of money would really help my family along", so, with this goal in mind, I began researching and investing in various different fields; from stocks to bonds to real estate to swing trading, and so on! My journey has been far from easy, but every step along the way has been incredibly rewarding as I've continued to learn about investing and building my wealth. Now, whilst making money is still a priority/hobby for me, having time with my family is what really matters - and is ultimately more satisfying than reaching any arbitrary figure.

Once I had achieved my goal of amassing a million dollars, it was not that such an amount was not enough; on the contrary, it is certainly a significant sum, and having so much money at once gave me a feeling of great accomplishment. However, I found that I didn't want to stop there. It wasn't just about wanting to make more money; it was about wanting to keep on experiencing the joy and sense of fulfilment from investing. As a youth, I had the dream of being rich and financially free, but with more experience, I now invest because I've learnt to love it! After sixteen years of engaging in this activity, I had finally come up with a system which enabled me to make consistent wins with most forms of investing. So, I figured, why should I let this newfound understanding go to waste? Why should I stop now when things were going so well?

When I decided to start learning about investing, I made sure that I was as prepared and organized as possible. I researched thoroughly, making notes on who offered the best services, the cheapest rates, and which brokerages had a reputation for being trustworthy. As someone who is naturally meticulous, it only made sense to take an in-depth approach to this as well. So, I made sticky notes, wrote in journals, and took copious notes in Word documents - all with the intention of compiling my thoughts throughout the process. Fast forward sixteen years later and here I am writing a series of books based on my experiences!

To ensure accuracy when writing this series from different perspectives - such as in 'Investing for Women' - I asked friends and fellow investors for their input to add further insight into each book. In fact, much of what is written regarding investing has been pre-written by me over time in various forms - be it a scribbled note or a more detailed outline of what I personally needed to know to invest in that field. Although not an expert in all areas of investment, through years of research and experience (and help from others!) I have been able to piece together content that reflects a diverse range of perspectives within this field.

Overall, this series of books is an amalgamation of much of my own research and experiences - some of which I have been continuing the entire time – others of which I've found either not profitable, or only mildly profitable, and so I've ditched them in favour of the better-earning ones! I have also included the thoughts, opinions and input from others involved in the investing world, to ensure accurate representation from a variety of perspectives. It has been a fun journey putting together all the pieces and rewarding at the same time. I am excited to share my knowledge and insight into investing with you all.

This series of handbooks provides a comprehensive guide for even the most beginner investor who is looking to start investing with confidence and ease. Each book dives deep into different aspects of investing, providing readers with the essential knowledge and information they need to make smart decisions when it comes to managing their money. These books are tailored specifically for those who want to gain a better understanding of investing in the financial markets and successfully managing their portfolios over time. Despite my American-based viewpoint, anyone can follow the principles explained within these pages regardless of their country. By reading this series from beginning to end, readers will be equipped with all the key tools necessary for success in investing and achieving long-term financial independence.

In addition to straightforward advice on how to invest, this series also offers guidance on everything from basic stock market terminology to more complex financial instruments. Readers will learn about diversification, risk management strategies, cost/benefit analysis, taxes related to investments, and more – giving them a strong foundation of knowledge that can be applied no matter what type of investment they choose.

My goal is for readers not only to understand what's going on in the markets but also to gain insight into why certain strategies have been useful for me, and how you can find the ones that suit you best.

Note:

I'm often asked what investments I'm presently making and it's an important question for those who are seeking to find financial freedom. After giving the matter a great deal of thought, I felt writing this information down in a book would quickly become outdated since I tend to rebalance my investments at least every three months. To provide readers with more up-to-date information, I decided to create a website which will help them understand what I am doing and encourage them to do the same. This website will not only provides details of the investments but also includes facts and figures that illustrate how these strategies can help people achieve their financial objectives. It will offer guidance on how to make wise investment choices and gives insight into the kinds of risk associated with each decision. Furthermore, this website contains detailed advice on how to maximize returns by diversifying your portfolio across multiple asset classes, mitigating losses through careful analysis of market trends, as well as other long-term strategies for achieving financial independence. By taking advantage of all the knowledge provided on this site, readers can feel confident that they have taken steps towards attaining their own financial freedom.

The journey to uncovering the secrets of successful investing can seem daunting, but I'm determined to make it easier for you! By subscribing to my email list, you'll stay up-to-date with the latest books in the series, and eventually be the first to know about my unique investment system. By being on the e-mail list I will also let you know when the website is launched too – exciting! I am constantly thinking "I wish I'd had this when I started! I'd have saved a decade worth of time!"

So, no matter your level of financial literacy, I have comprehensive information for anyone who is keen on learning more. With an array of resources at my disposal, I can give you an in-depth look at the foundation of successful investing. Through these materials, I will provide a thorough look into elements such as risk management principles and best practices, financial forecasting, budgeting techniques, and so much more.

On top of this knowledge base, subscribers will also be given access to exclusive tools such as calculators and other interactive features that can help simplify complex topics like portfolio construction. This way, no matter what your individual goals are when it comes to building wealth through investments - I'm here to help!

By joining my email list you'll have access to all these resources and more. So come on board for this exciting adventure and discover how you can get started investing for success today!

So, with no further ado, let's dive in!

Your Free Bonus Gifts

Accelerate Your **Learning**

Maximize Your **Earning**

We are here to help you crush it – no bones about it. To make the most of this book, there are two things you'll need:

1. **FREE RESOURCES**

   We have created a number of free resources for you to take advantage of. Use them to accelerate your learning and maximize your earning!

2. **FURTHER RESOURCES**

   We are constantly striving to continue supporting both our team and our students. We are busy creating a website to better highlight all of our investing tips, tricks and current holdings to help our users better see what we're actually up to! To find out when we launch this, and be alerted when we release other titles, just subscribe to our e-mail list and you'll be the first to know!

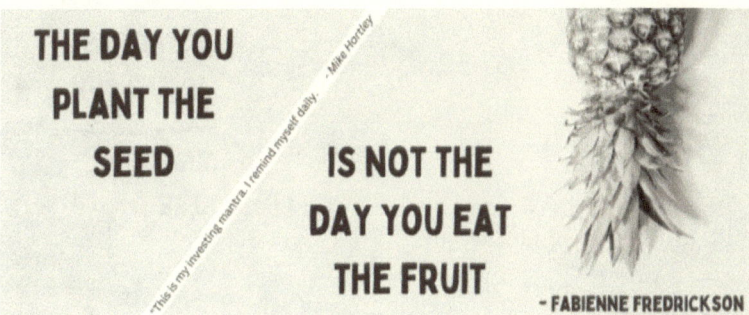

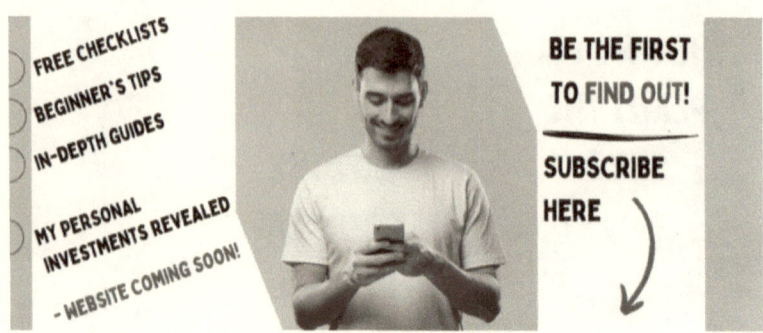

Subscribe To The Newsletter and Join Us!

- Find out the secrets to investing safely
- Join the growing **FIRE** (**F**inancially **I**ndependent **R**etire **E**arly) Movement!
- Live your passive income lifestyle…

www.thefirefund.com/free-gift

Table of Contents

Introduction

If you do not find a way to make money while you sleep,
you will work till you die.

–Warren Buffet

Money is made by consistently leveraging time, skills, and resources in the form of goods and services in exchange for currency.

This basic understanding is the difference between where you are now and where you want to be. It is the difference between zero and a million dollars, and between a person who works three jobs to make a six-figure annual income and another person making the same amount of money from one or two businesses they run right from their home computer in a matter of months.

> Working from home can be great, but it doesn't mean you're making passive income.

Passive income is making money on autopilot or using money to make money. A passive income stream can be a financial investment with periodic returns or a business that leverages goods and services to generate cash.

The question you might be asking yourself right now is, "How?" In this book, we will be focusing on the goldmine: real estate.

Over the years, one of the fastest-growing industries has been real estate. Since the early 1900s, when the National Association of Real Estate Boards started to promote the idea that every American should own their own home, the industry has experienced its fair share of ups and downs. Until 1934, when this campaign started, most Americans were home renters, and they did not see a problem with it. But when the Federal Housing Administration (FHA) began providing flexible insurance plans to enable ordinary citizens to purchase their "dream homes" by making a down payment and spreading the rest over a few years (with interest), the surge for homeownership rose (Ancestry, 2017).

Understand this—where there is demand, there must be supply. As the surge in homeownership increased, people sought to turn it into a business—leveraging their time, knowledge, or resources for money. As such, the real estate business in America has a rich and inspiring history. From the country's earliest days, people have been buying, selling, and building properties. The industry has undergone many changes over the years, but one thing has remained constant: the American dream of owning a home.

As the decades passed, the real estate industry continued to evolve. The rise of technology and the internet has made it easier to find and purchase a property, and the industry has become increasingly globalized. Today, real estate professionals use cutting-edge tools and techniques to market properties, and buyers and sellers can access a wealth of information online.

Despite the changes in the industry, the American dream of homeownership remains as strong as ever. For many people, owning a home is not just a financial investment but also a symbol of success, stability, and the American way of life. Real estate professionals play a vital role in helping people achieve this dream, and the industry continues to be a significant driver of economic growth and prosperity.

Buying and selling properties is not the only way to enter the real estate industry. In recent years, people have made a business out of renting short-term properties to tenants who need places to stay for a predetermined amount of time. These days, you don't even need to own a property to start short-term renting. All you need to do is find a lovely house or apartment in a great area and gain the landlord's permission to sublet it. It's as simple as that.

> Starting and running a successful Airbnb business can be a great way to earn extra income and potentially turn it into a full-time job.

However, it can also be challenging and complex, especially if you have little to no experience with real estate. In this guide, we will provide a comprehensive introduction to the world of Airbnb, covering everything from setting up your listing, creating a solid marketing strategy, managing your guests, and maintaining your property, to scaling it up and turning it into a full-time job.

Before we introduce to you what we will be covering in this

book, we must reestablish that every business requires the owner to possess a particular mindset. You cannot fear having new people stay at your property and expect to make any money. You also cannot treat people with little or no regard and hope to make good profits. In this day and age, businesses thrive on word of mouth, positive reviews, and referrals. This does not mean that there are no other ways to make it in this business, but we must establish that the key ingredient in making your business prosper is you.

First, we will review the basics of finding a suitable property and setting up your listing. Not all properties are "good" for business, and we will explain why later in this book. A good listing includes a detailed and accurate description of your property, as well as high-quality photos that will make your listing stand out. A well-written and detailed description of your property will help potential guests understand what they can expect from your listing, and high-quality photos will give them a sense of what the property looks like. It's also important to be honest and transparent about the property, including any potential downsides or limitations.

Next, we will deal with pricing. When it comes to pricing, you'll want to be competitive and ensure you're getting a fair return for your property. It is vital to research similar listings in your area to get a sense of the going rates and be sure to factor in any additional costs like cleaning or maintenance. You should also be flexible with your pricing and be willing to adjust it based on demand, seasonality, and other factors.

Once you've set up your listing, it's time to start marketing it to potential guests. Building a solid online presence is vital to attracting more guests and bookings. This includes creating a website, leveraging social media, and building a network of satisfied guests who will leave positive reviews and recommend your property to others. Social media platforms like Facebook, Instagram, and Twitter can be great ways to reach a broad audience, and you can also use them to connect with potential guests and answer any questions they may have. Additionally, having a website can provide more information about your property and also help with Search Engine Optimization (SEO), making it easier to find your listing in search engines.

Once you start getting bookings, it's essential to be prepared for your guests' arrival. This includes ensuring that your property is clean and well-maintained, providing clear instructions for check-in and check-out, and being available to answer any questions or concerns. It's also important to be flexible and accommodating to any changes, such as last-minute cancellations or property damage.

Managing your guests is just as important as managing your property. One of the most important things is to set clear house rules and make sure that your guests are aware of them before they arrive. Providing amenities and extras that will make their stay more comfortable, like fresh linens, toiletries, and a fully stocked kitchen, can also go a long way in creating a positive experience for your guests. Being responsive to any feedback or complaints is also crucial, and addressing any issues as soon as they come up will help ensure that your guests have a great stay. If you have perhaps already started or tried.

Maintaining your property is also crucial to running a successful Airbnb business. This includes regular cleaning and upkeep, as well as keeping an eye out for any repairs or upgrades that may be necessary. It would help if you were also mindful of the style and design of your property, as it can significantly impact how your guests perceive it and their overall experience. Creating a comfortable and welcoming atmosphere and making your property stand out from the competition is a way to keep your guests coming back and attract new ones.

If you want to grow your Airbnb business, scaling it up and turning it into a full-time job is a great option. This includes hiring staff, creating a website, and creating a genuine brand.

This book is not just a guide on how to make money. It is an in-depth guide to the basic and complex workings of a successful Airbnb business. Turn the page to start this new journey with us.

CHAPTER 1

Understanding Airbnb

My rich dad taught me to focus on passive income and spend my time acquiring the assets that provide passive or long-term residual income...passive income from capital gains, dividends, residual income from the business, rental income from real estate, and royalties.

–Robert Kiyosaki

Understanding is the foundation of proper implementation, which in turn is the foundation of consistent and improving results. It's not enough to obtain properties and offer short-term stays at "good" prices.

> To run an Airbnb business and be good at it, you need to know and understand the basics.

Sometimes even the most obvious information could be exactly what you need to make your big break.

In this chapter, you will learn what exactly Airbnb is and how it works. You are reading this book because you want to make more money, so yes, we will be discussing the process, pros, and cons of investing in Airbnb. Understandably, it can be a bit unnerving to have people staying on your property, especially if you also live there, so we'll talk about hosting and address a few rumors you may have heard online. In a nutshell, we will be talking about Airbnb as a business and how it compares to other streams of passive income.

Let's get started!

The Evolution of Bed-and-Breakfasts

While many of us may be familiar with the more recent twin (I'm talking about Airbnb), the concept of bed-and-breakfasts (B&Bs) has spanned generations, years before anyone even thought about the name Airbnb. Bed-and-breakfasts have a rich history dating back to early 19th century in Europe and have continued to span centuries and spread beyond the borders of Europe to across the world.

What emerged from a simple idea of serving travelers in Europe with a simple lodging option and feeding them has now grown into a thriving industry that serves not just travelers anymore but a wide range of guests in several places worldwide. In this article, we'll explore the evolution of B&Bs and how they've changed to meet the needs of travelers over time.

What Is a Bed-and-Breakfast?

Bed-and-breakfasts are a type of accommodation that offers overnight stays for individuals needing a place to spend the night. The exciting thing about this accommodation is that it has breakfast in the morning. I know you may be wondering how this differs from traditional hotels. Well, unlike more commercial hotels, bed-and-breakfasts take a more personal approach to how they take care of their guests. Usually, B&Bs are owned and operated by the homeowner, who stays on the premises with the guests, and most of the properties used for B&Bs have an intimate and homely touch compared to hotels. So, guests not only get a great place to sleep, but they also get a great breakfast and an experience similar to being in their own homes.

B&Bs can be found in various settings, such as rural farms, historic homes, urban townhouses, and beachfront cottages. Not all B&Bs are the same. Some offer only a few of their rooms for rent, while others may have several rooms or even entire guest houses available for rent. One of the most appealing aspects of a B&B is the personalized attention and service that guests receive. Unlike hotels, which can feel impersonal, B&Bs are lauded for the several ways they offer a warm and welcoming environment to their guests. Some B&Bs provide recommendations to local restaurants and the available side attractions in the area, while others provide customized breakfast options for guests who have dietary restrictions. B&B owners go above and beyond to make their guests feel at home.

Another advantage of staying at a B&B is the opportunity to experience the local culture and community. Many B&Bs are located in residential neighborhoods or on historic properties, offering a glimpse into the local way of life. Guests can interact with locals, learn about the area's history, culture, and get a sense of living in that particular town or city.

The Early Days of B&Bs

B&Bs have existed since the Middle Ages, and this is the earliest history of B&Bs. In those days, travelers who journeyed from one city to another would often need places to rest their heads, and given the fact that there were no hotels or inns then, they had to take residence in private homes and monasteries.

During the early years, people traveling would either take up residence in private homes or do so at no cost. Then the arrangement was usually based on social status, and wealthy people were more likely to open up their homes to other rich people like them, knowing fully well that the gesture would be repaid when the need arose. It was a way of strengthening bonds and extending hospitality to others who were considered to be similar to them.

However, in the 18th century, Europe, specifically the UK. Travelers at the time would stay at inns, which were expensive, overcrowded, and unhygienic. This led to the emergence of private homes offering lodging and breakfast to travelers. These lodgings were known as "boarding houses" or "lodging houses." The appeal of these lodgings was in the low prices and also the hospitality guests received from the homeowners, and this made more and more people choose them over traditional hotels and motels.

It was not until the 19th century, in the British Isles, that these private homes began to be referred to as "bed-and-breakfasts" or "B&Bs." These private lodgings were typically run by families who rented out rooms to travelers and often included a home-cooked breakfast. They usually placed signs outside their doors and windows to let tourists and travelers know their property was open for rent. B&Bs were then known for their personalized service and friendly hosts, and they quickly became popular with travelers looking for a more homely experience than traditional hotels and inns.

The wave of B&Bs soon spread to the United States in the 19th century during the era of the Great Depression. Then things got increasingly hard, and many people could not afford to maintain their standard of living. So many families opened their houses to travelers who would pay them for the night. This allowed families to earn extra income and helped travelers cut down on the costs of renting a hotel. The guests would get a place to sleep and also receive breakfast in the mornings before they headed out.

Bed-and-Breakfasts in the 20th Century

When the Second World War ended, and people began traveling all over the world again, B&Bs became even more popular, and unlike before, when families did B&Bs to bring in extra cash, many started seeing this as a viable business idea that could be pursued full time. This brought about a renaissance of B&Bs.

This coincided with the departure of young people from the US to Europe. Many of them, who had traveled to Europe for either schooling or tourist visits and who got first-hand experience of the B&B culture in Europe, brought this business model back to America. They began establishing their own B&Bs all over the United States. This led many homeowners with large homes or historic properties to open their doors to travelers, offering them a more personal and unique experience than traditional hotels. The beauty of these homes and the hospitality provided by the homeowners made B&Bs the best option for tourists and travelers.

As the years progressed, B&Bs became a better option for travelers as they were cheaper and more homely, and guests got everything they wanted. At this time, most B&Bs had simple amenities that catered to the client's immediate needs. A typical B&B offers guests a comfortable bed and a simple breakfast. Guests would have to share a bathroom, but as popularity grew and the demand for B&Bs increased, the operators of B&Bs knew that things had to change if they wanted to keep attracting guests.

The world was increasingly changing by the day. New technologies were springing up, and people's tastes were gradually changing and evolving with the times, and many owners knew they had to step up their game if they still wanted to retain their clients. Unlike guests from the early days of B&Bs, guests nowadays want more than just a comfortable bed and a home-cooked breakfast. The world in which B&Bs originated was simpler compared to the 20th century world. Guests who lodged in B&Bs wanted a nice and cheap place to spend the night but amenities that would allow them to function in the world. No one would like to go to a lodge where they do not have access to cell reception or an internet connection. This brought about the inclusion of private bathrooms, air conditioning, and an internet connection in the lodgings. Many operators of B&Bs started offering their guests private bathrooms and stable internet connections, and some included air conditioners and even televisions in the rooms. Thus, making

B&Bs a real home away from home.

Bed-and-Breakfasts in the 21st Century

As the years passed, the world kept changing, and guests' needs kept evolving. Many B&Bs expanded their services to include a range of amenities, such as high-speed internet connections, on-site spas, farm-to-table dining experiences, and concierge services. Additionally, many B&Bs decided to adopt a different business model that catered to a specific market. Several B&Bs opened up only to guests like eco-tourists, LGBTQ+ travelers, or adventure seekers. These B&Bs tailored their services to fit the needs of their guests, which allowed them to have a constant pool of guests. For instance, B&Bs for LGBTQ+ travelers offered a safe space for their guests and had shows and side attractions specifically catered to members of the LGBTQ+ community. They also became sites of romantic getaways for gay couples without fear of discrimination or censorship.

In recent years, we have seen the emergence of luxury B&Bs that offer a higher-end experience, often with more advanced technology and unique services and experiences. These B&Bs often offer a riveting atmosphere, trading the old, homely feel for more stylish decor and providing access to personalized services. Some of these B&Bs have incorporated learning experiences for their guests by organizing cooking or art classes for the guests, wine-tasting events, and other regular workshops.

Furthermore, the B&B industry has adapted to the constant change in technology and people's travel choices. Unlike before, when guests did not see the lodge they wanted to rent until they arrived, with the internet and social media, potential guests can scout the B&Bs they are interested in before making payment. Many B&Bs now have websites and social media accounts where travelers can easily make reservations for the accommodations and learn more about the property before they arrive. With social media reviews, people can know what to expect, thereby allowing them to make an informed choice about where to stay.

Some B&Bs have adopted similar technologies used in hotels, such as mobile check-in and keyless entry, thereby simplifying the check-in process and reducing stress for the guests. Some have even begun incorporating innovative home technology, such as voice-activated assistants that allow guests to control the temperature in their room, the lighting, and other amenities with just their voice or a mobile app.

There is no denying that as the travel industry continues to evolve, so will the bed-and-breakfast industry. To remain relevant, many B&Bs are adapting to the constant change in the world, and many are becoming concerned with sustainability and eco-friendliness, with a focus on using local and organic products in the services they render.

In conclusion, the evolution of bed-and-breakfasts has been significant, from its humble beginnings in the Middle Ages as a spare bedroom in a private home to the luxurious properties that can be found today. Driven by the changing needs and preferences of travelers, as well as advances in technology and the broader hospitality industry, what started as a simple lodging option has transformed into an industry that offers a range of amenities and services to meet the needs of today's travelers.

However, one unchanging fact is the personalized service and friendly hosts that have made B&Bs so popular over the years.

As the travel industry continues to change, it will be interesting to see how the B&B industry adapts to meet the needs and expectations of travelers. One thing is sure, however: The B&B industry will continue to provide a unique and personalized travel experience for those in need.

What Is Airbnb?

Airbnb is a technology-based platform that connects travelers seeking unique and local travel experiences with hosts willing to rent their homes, apartments, or rooms. The company has been instrumental in revolutionizing the way people travel and stay in different places around the world" (Guttentag, 2017).

Airbnb is short for "Air bed-and-breakfast." It is a vacation rental company owned by Nathan Blecharczyk, Joe Gebbia, and Brian Chesky. The company runs a website that links individuals needing a place to stay with those who have a spare room or property available for rent (or to sublet). The company was established in 2008, with its headquarters in San Francisco, California. It has become one of the most well-known and commonly utilized short-term rental sites (Aiyden, 2019).

To properly understand what Airbnb is, we would have to describe the term from two perspectives—the property owner/lessor (the host) and the customer (the guest). From the customer's perspective, we can describe Airbnb as a service that provides a list of available apartments or houses, they can rent for the duration of their stay in whatever location they choose. The guests can choose a place based on their preferences, e.g., size, number of rooms, unique amenities, pricing, etc. The term "Airbnb" is also used to describe the properties themselves after they have been listed on the website, so we can also describe Airbnb as a house or apartment that a guest can rent for a short while for a price set by the host.

If you are looking to go into the Airbnb business, it would be a business opportunity where you provide spaces or properties for people looking for a place to stay for a while. A guest's stay can range from one night to a couple of months, depending on the individual, and you get to charge them per night. Airbnb works like a hotel but without the formalities of running a large-scale business in just one location.

One of the most significant advantages of the Airbnb business over running a hotel is that you can offer apartments in several locations worldwide. The best part about this is that you don't even need to own any of these properties!

How Does It Work?

- **Signing up**: To get started on Airbnb, guests, and hosts need to create an account. They'll need to provide basic information, like their name, email address, and payment details.

- **Listing**: If you're a host, you'll need to list your property on Airbnb by providing information such as the location, number of rooms, and photos. This will help guests find your property and see what it looks like.

- **Booking**: Once a guest finds a property they like, they can make a booking request. The host will receive a notification and can accept or decline the request. If the request is accepted, the guest's payment will be securely processed through Airbnb, and the host will receive compensation 24 hours after the guest has checked in.

- **Staying**: During the stay, the host is responsible for providing a clean and safe property, while the guest is responsible for following the rules and respecting the property. Airbnb provides a messaging system for guests and hosts to communicate before and during their stay.

- **Reviewing**: After the stay, both the guest and the host can leave a review of each other. This helps build trust within the Airbnb community and ensures everyone has a positive experience.

  To be successful on Airbnb, it's crucial to provide high-quality accommodations, be responsive to guests' requests and questions, and create a welcoming and comfortable environment.

Hosts should also ensure their listings are accurate and up-to-date and keep their properties clean and well-maintained. For guests, it's essential to read the descriptions and reviews of properties before booking and to communicate clearly with the host about their needs and expectations.

Is Airbnb Safe for Investment?

The short answer is "yes."

For various reasons, Airbnb is regarded as a risk-free investment. First, the platform has a significant and increasing user base, with millions of individuals booking short-term rentals through the site. This implies that homes listed on the marketplace are in great demand, and hosts should expect a continuous stream of reservations.

Furthermore, with features such as verified listings, guest reviews, and a secure payment mechanism, Airbnb has a reputation for offering a safe and secure booking experience. The company also has an excellent financial position, thanks to considerable venture capital investment and a successful initial public offering in 2020. The market is likely to expand more in the coming years due to factors such as increased travel and urbanization.

According to recent studies, the future of Airbnb looks very promising. In a report by Statista, it was estimated that the global vacation rental market would reach $96.85 billion by 2023. Increasing demand for affordable and flexible travel options drives this growth (Statista, n.d.).

Airbnb can be considered a safe investment due to its stable financial performance and high demand for alternative forms of accommodation. However, it is crucial to evaluate potential risks, such as changes in regulations and market conditions" (Rosen & Kim, 2019).

Another critical factor that will impact the future of Airbnb is the increasing trend of sustainable tourism. More and more travelers are looking for eco-friendly and sustainable travel options, and Airbnb has responded to this trend by introducing green initiatives, such as the "Green Rewards" program, which provides discounts to hosts who adopt sustainable practices.

However, the future of Airbnb is not without challenges. One of the biggest challenges the company faces is regulation. Airbnb has faced opposition from traditional hotels and other travel companies, and many cities have introduced rules to limit the number of short-term rentals. In addition, the company has faced criticism for not doing enough to prevent illegal activities, such as parties, on its platform.

Despite these challenges, Airbnb remains optimistic about its future. The company is continuously improving its platform and expanding its offerings, such as by introducing its luxury vacation rental platform, "Luxury Retreats." Furthermore, Airbnb is expanding into new markets and working with local communities to impact local economies positively.

The Truth About Hosting

There is a ton of information in circulation about Airbnb hosting. There are a lot of people who have been in this business for a couple of years, made a decent amount of money, and are now going around calling for students while shoving the amount of money they have made and how many properties they have listed in your face.

Ignore the dollar signs.

If there are two truths you need to know before joining the bandwagon, the first is that you need to understand that the Airbnb business, just like every other legitimate business in existence, is not a get-rich-quick scheme. People tend to think that just because the company has a low barrier to entry, it must be easy, and they don't have to do any research. If you are not ready to work, you might quit now.

The second is that you would need to study and understand the market and evolve as it changes. If you are unable to do this, you will be left behind. As such, no one formula will work forever. You also have to start thinking like a business owner. You cannot just clean up your mom's basement, take some pictures, and list it on Airbnb, expecting to make some money. You have to be able to provide a fantastic customer experience. Get a list and write out what you would love to see in your rental apartment if you were a customer. This will help you with a strategy for design and presentation. Of course, different people have different likes and needs; that's where being flexible comes into play.

Another thing you need to know is that not all landlords will let you use their properties as a Short Term Rental (STR). Word of advice: *Do not try to do it undercover.* If it says "No Subletting" or "No Airbnb" on the property lease form, do not sign it. A landlord might ask for a percentage of your monthly earnings before you are allowed to list the property, and that's okay. Just make sure you have a written contract that clearly states the terms of the agreement. We also advise that you register your business as an LLC to have a formal contract with the landlord.

Lastly, it would help if you were ready to deal with people. Even if you're not a people person, the goal here is to make some money, right?

> So, sometimes you have to suck it up and put yourself out there.

You also have to be ready to deal with people's excesses. Guests can sometimes be unreasonable. You will meet a few people who will steal or damage your property for no reason or refuse to leave after the amount of time for which they were paid has expired. Sometimes you may even have to involve law enforcement. Don't get me wrong; not all guests are bad. You will meet many great people who will leave encouraging reviews and recommend your property to their friends. I'm just saying you have to be ready to accommodate and adjust when dealing with guests.

It's not all sunshine and rainbows, but it is worth it.

Myth Versus Reality

Myth 1: Hosting on Airbnb is easy and hassle-free.

Reality: Hosting on Airbnb requires a significant amount of effort and attention to detail, from preparing and listing the property to communicating with guests and maintaining the property.

Myth 2: Hosts make a lot of money on Airbnb.

Reality: While it is possible to make a good income on Airbnb, it varies considerably based on location, type of property, and time of year. Hosts must also take into account expenses such as cleaning and maintenance fees.

Myth 3: Guests will automatically love your property.

Reality: A sound review system is in place to help guests find high-quality properties, but it's not a guarantee. Hosts must ensure their property is well-maintained and equipped with all the necessary amenities to attract and retain guests.

Myth 4: Hosting on Airbnb is total passive income.

Reality: Hosting on Airbnb requires a significant amount of time and effort, from managing bookings and responding to guests' inquiries to preparing the property for their arrival.

Myth 5: Hosting on Airbnb does not require insurance.

Reality: Hosts are responsible for ensuring their property is adequately protected, and many countries require hosts to have insurance coverage. Hosts must understand their local regulations and ensure they have proper insurance coverage.

The Big Picture

Airbnb is the world's leading online marketplace for booking unique, short-term accommodations. Airbnb is a low-cost alternative to traditional hotel stays that allows travelers to live like a local in their chosen location. Airbnb, in addition to providing a platform for travelers, will also enable individuals and small businesses to monetize their unused spaces. Despite the criticism and regulatory challenges, Airbnb has continued to grow and innovate, introducing new services such as Luxe (Airbnb, 2019).

Evaluating Airbnb in Comparison to Its Competition

Airbnb is one of the most well-known and successful online marketplaces for short-term rentals, but it faces intense competition from several other players in the industry, such as Booking.com, Expedia, and Vrbo. Airbnb has been able to differentiate itself through its unique user experience that focuses on community and local experiences, as well as its extensive global reach (currently available in over 220 countries). However, these strengths have also become weaknesses as Airbnb has faced criticism over issues related to regulation, safety, and discrimination. Despite these challenges, Airbnb has continued to grow and expand, with a recent report estimating that the company's revenue will reach $9.5 billion by the end of 2023. While Airbnb certainly has its strengths and weaknesses, it remains a significant player in the short-term rental market and a key competitor for other players in the industry (Sun, 2022).

Pros and Cons of Investing in Airbnb

As with all business ventures, investing in Airbnb has upsides and downsides. These are serious factors to consider before diving in.

Upsides:

- Strong brand recognition and reputation.

- Broad reach and significant market share in the short-term rental industry.

- Growing demand for alternative and flexible accommodation options.

- Potential for high returns on investment.

- Robust technology and data capabilities to drive growth and innovation.

And now, the downsides:

- High level of competition from established players and new entrants.

- Regulatory and legal challenges, particularly around zoning and taxes.

- Concerns over the safety and security of both hosts and guests, especially in volatile areas.

- Vulnerability to economic downturns and changes in consumer behavior.

- Dependence on a small group of major markets for significant revenue.

It may also be helpful to consult with a financial advisor or conduct thorough research to fully understand the current market conditions and the company's financials.

Key Takeaways

- Airbnb is a profitable business venture with a low barrier to entry into the market.

- You do not have to own a property to get started.

- To succeed at Airbnb, your properties and listings must be guest-centered.

- There is legal work involved, such as registering your business, getting property insurance, and paying taxes.

- The ability to manage guests properly is critical.

What Next?

If you're planning to go into the Airbnb business, even if you are not ready, you can get started by:

- Registering your STR business as an LLC

- Do research on properties in your area or consider hiring a property manager to find some good options

- Do market research and find out what's trending, and what other hosts are doing.

The next chapter is going to be all about you!

As a host, the right mindset can turn the bleakest situation into a profitable, long-term relationship. Turn the page, and let's talk about it.

CHAPTER 2

Creating Your Hosting Mindset

Entertaining doesn't need to be a difficult or daunting process. Throwing an unforgettable party doesn't require a ton of time or money; it just requires a little thought, creativity, and heart.

–Maury Ankrum

Here are the two lessons this chapter is based on: *Fear* and *intimidation* are two things you will never need; all the big-shot Airbnb owners are guest-centered. Nobody likes the bare minimum. Especially when they're paying for it. Why would anyone pay for the same things they can get at home? Do you know what kids call that these days?

Basic.

If guests want nothing but the necessities, they will stay at inns. I served milk because I like milk. In chapter one, we focused on creating the ultimate guest experience. In chapter two, we will discuss just how to do that. First, we will discuss the mindset of a successful host, which is themed around hospitality. We will also talk about one of the main ingredients of success, which is the passion for succeeding. We will also talk about the two types of profit that come from satisfied guests, and lastly, we will discuss everything you need to consider before becoming an Airbnb host.

Pay attention as we unlock the secrets to exceptional hosting and discover the power of a positive mindset.

Setting a Hosting Mindset

The hosting mindset of a successful Airbnb host prioritizes the comfort and satisfaction of guests while also embracing continuous learning and growth. This mindset includes qualities such as positivity, proactivity, open-mindedness, attention to detail, clear communication, and a focus on creating a welcoming environment. A successful host views hosting as an opportunity to provide a memorable experience for guests rather than just a means to make money. They approach challenges with a solution-oriented attitude and continuously strive to improve their hosting skills and guest satisfaction. By adopting this hosting mindset, Airbnb hosts can ensure a positive and successful hosting experience.

According to Smith and Jones (2020), having a hospitality mindset means embracing the values of generosity, kindness, and a genuine desire to serve others. This mindset is essential for individuals and organizations in the hospitality industry to create memorable experiences and foster lasting relationships with guests. Brown and Green (2022) supported this claim by stating that adopting a hospitality mindset means embracing the importance of creating welcoming and memorable experiences for guests. This includes putting the needs and desires of the guest first, being proactive in addressing any issues that may arise, and going above and beyond to create a positive impression.

The right mindset is crucial if you hope to make it big in the Airbnb business. You may have to learn, unlearn, and relearn some things, but everything pays off in the long run. Having the right mindset is important so that you can handle your guests. It will help if you have the right attitude when dealing with landlords, vendors, and workers or staff.

Having a Hospitality Mindset

A hospitality mindset as an Airbnb host is crucial for success in the sharing economy. It means that the host approaches hosting with a focus on providing a welcoming, comfortable, and memorable experience for guests. This mindset sets the foundation for building positive relationships with guests and creating a profitable and sustainable Airbnb business.

The first aspect of a hospitality mindset is providing a clean and well-maintained space. A guest's first impression of the room will shape their overall experience and could potentially impact their decision to book again or recommend the property to others. Regular cleaning and maintenance, such as replacing linens, fixing any broken items, and ensuring that the space is free of any clutter, are essential to maintaining a high standard of quality for guests.

Another critical aspect of a hospitality mindset is attention to detail. This includes providing guests with fresh towels, clean bed linens, and basic toiletries. In addition, hosts can also offer additional touches such as fresh flowers, a welcome note, or a small snack to make guests feel unique and valued. These small gestures can make a significant impact in terms of guest satisfaction and the overall experience.

Effective communication is also an essential component of a hospitality mindset. Hosts should be available to respond to guests' questions and concerns promptly and professionally. This can be done through Airbnb's messaging platform or other communication methods such as email or phone. By being responsive and helpful, hosts can build trust with guests and create a more positive experience.

A warm and welcoming environment is also a vital aspect of a hospitality mindset. Hosts should aim to create a comfortable and inviting space, which can be achieved through thoughtful decor, lighting, and ambient music. In addition, providing guests with a tour of the room and offering local recommendations can help guests feel more at home and enhance their overall experience.

Finally, a hospitality mindset also involves anticipating guests' needs and going the extra mile to exceed their expectations. This can include providing guests with a list of local attractions or restaurants, offering to arrange transportation, or providing additional amenities such as a yoga mat or a portable speaker. By providing exceptional service and going above and beyond, hosts can create loyal customers who will return again and again.

In conclusion, having a hospitality mindset as an Airbnb host is essential for success in the sharing economy. By providing a clean and well-maintained space, attention to detail, effective communication, a warm and welcoming environment, and anticipating guests' needs, hosts can create positive relationships with guests, enhance their overall experience, and build a profitable and sustainable Airbnb business.

Have a Passion for Succeeding

Passion is the driving force that keeps entrepreneurs motivated and committed to their goals, even when faced with challenges and obstacles.

> As an Airbnb business owner, you must be passionate about providing a unique and memorable experience to your guests.

You should have the desire to create a welcoming and comfortable environment for them and be willing to go above and beyond to ensure their stay is memorable.

Additionally, having a passion for the business side of things is equally important. You should be dedicated to continuously improving your property, maximizing your earnings, and staying up-to-date on industry trends and best practices. It would help if you were willing to invest time and resources into marketing, customer service, and financial management.

Ultimately, having a passion for success as an Airbnb business owner means that you are willing to work hard, embrace challenges, and never give up on your goals. With a combination of dedication, hard work, and a passion for success, you can achieve great things as an Airbnb business owner. Whether you are just starting or have been in the business for years, maintaining your passion for success is essential for long-term success and growth in the competitive and ever-evolving world of short-term rentals.

Satisfied Guests Means Profit

Guest satisfaction is a crucial factor in determining a hotel's profitability, as satisfied guests are more likely to return and recommend the hotel to others. Furthermore, positive word-of-mouth promotion generated by happy guests can lead to increased demand for the hotel's services and higher occupancy rates" (Kim & Lee, 2018). Customers are the lifeblood of every business. The number of paying guests that come through your business each month determines your monthly profit.

Two types of profits come from satisfied guests:

1. **Instant Profit**: This refers to the money you make when a customer books and pays for your property for some time. It's the money you make per customer that books your Airbnb.

2. **Future Profit**: Future profit is any money that comes from referrals and word of mouth. In terms of future profit, we can talk about three streams:

o The chance for a revisit: If a customer likes the experience your property provides, there is a big chance that they will book you again whenever they need an Airbnb in that location again. Sometimes, guests stick with a particular host once they see that you can consistently provide the experience required.

o The chance for positive reviews: Positive reviews are everything for properties on Airbnb. Checking reviews is an important step when guests are choosing a property. If there's one thing that customers tend to do, it's talk. And wouldn't it be better to say only good things about your property? It's also not a bad idea to encourage guests to leave positive reviews if they love staying on your property.

o The chance for recommendation: How many items have you bought, and how many places have you visited, just because someone recommended them? Funny enough, people don't only take recommendations from their friends or family. They can find suggestions and opinions online. Do not doubt the power of positive reviews. Sometimes one satisfied customer can be the key to lots of repeat business.

Don't only strive to get people to leave positive reviews on your listing, strive to exceed the expectations of every customer you get. This will not only incentivize people to refer you but also bring you long-term repeat business. Also, don't be scared to get creative. What you are selling is not exactly a place to stay. It's a beautiful experience.

This is the key to being overbooked.

Things to Consider Before Becoming an Airbnb Host

- **Local laws and regulations**: Ensure you understand the rules and regulations for hosting guests in your area, including taxes, zoning, and insurance requirements.

- **Insurance**: Consider purchasing insurance to protect yourself and your property from potential damages or liability claims.

- **Cleaning and maintenance**: Plan for the time and cost of cleaning and maintaining your property, as well as providing fresh linens and towels for guests.

- **Safety**: Ensure your property is safe for guests by checking smoke detectors, installing carbon monoxide detectors, and having a fire extinguisher on hand.

- **Amenities**: Decide what amenities to offer, such as Wi-Fi, cable TV, kitchen supplies, etc., and ensure they are in good working condition.

- **Guest communication**: Be prepared to communicate with guests before, during, and after their stay to answer questions, provide information, and resolve any issues.

- **Pricing strategy**: Determine a fair price for your property based on market demand, location, and the amenities and services you offer.

- **Guest expectations**: Consider what guests expect from your property and their experience, and plan accordingly.

- **Availability**: Decide when your property will be available for guests and how you will handle booking requests.

- **Guest reviews**: Be aware that guest reviews can impact your reputation and future bookings, so it's crucial to provide a positive and memorable experience for guests.

Key Takeaways

Here are the essential points from Chapter 2:

- The mindset of a successful host is centered on hospitality and a positive guest experience.

- To make it in the Airbnb business, you must have a passion for succeeding.

- Satisfied customers bring instant profit and set you up for future gain.

- Don't be afraid to charge a reasonable amount per night. Low prices don't always attract guests.

What Next?

Here are some steps you can take right now to put yourself on the right path to a successful Airbnb business:

- Check out a few listings in your area and compare them with the reviews they've gotten. Also, compare them with other listings to find out what types of listings have the best reviews.

- Read books on hospitality and interpersonal relationships.

- Practice being more hospitable than the people around you.

In the next chapter, we will discuss the importance and process of finding the perfect properties to list.

CHAPTER 3

Choosing Your One

With real estate, it's location, location, location.

–Christopher Buckley

Great aesthetics and luxury amenities will all go to waste if your Airbnb is in the wrong place. What is the first thing you think about when you want to take a vacation? You decide on a place. The location is a huge factor when planning or taking a trip. It is the one factor that influences your activities, the length of your stay, your budget, etc.

Remember that we must look at things from our guests' points of view. If we can note all the factors that influence a guest's choice of property, we can tailor our properties to suit our ideal guest's needs.

In this chapter, we will discover how to identify the right property for you by revealing the types of Airbnb businesses and the importance of a good location. We will also talk about value propositions and the process of listing a property on Airbnb. This chapter will be especially beneficial to people who have already started their businesses but are not making any money or are looking to make more money.

Identify the Right Airbnb for You

My dad used to say, "When choosing a house to rent or buy, you have to look at the location in terms of proximity to school, church, health care, and markets." We're not buying a house, but the same rule applies when choosing a property to list. However, selecting properties based on proximity and access to certain places depends on the priorities of the individual guest.

For example, a tourist would want an Airbnb close to the town center to access the sites they'd like to visit easily. Honeymooners may prefer a serene area with lots of greenery and nature. Corporate executives would choose an Airbnb with a workspace. So in identifying the right Airbnb for you, it's advisable to "niche down," that is, discover who your ideal guest is and tailor the designs and aesthetics of your property to suit their needs.

Now, let us discuss the types of Airbnb businesses according to the types of properties:

- **Traditional Vacation Rentals**: This is the most common type of Airbnb rental, where a host rents out their entire property or a private room to travelers. Examples include a beach house, a city apartment, or a mountain cabin.

- **Unique Spaces**: These are unusual or one-of-a-kind spaces, such as treehouses, yurts, houseboats, and castles. They offer a more unique and memorable travel experience.

- **Alternative Accommodations**: This category includes unique spaces like RVs, tents, and glamping tents set up in the great outdoors.

- **B&Bs**: A bed-and-breakfast is a traditional accommodation where the owner provides a private room and serves breakfast. Airbnb offers B&Bs as a separate category to make it easier for travelers to find this type of accommodation.

- **Boutique Hotels**: Airbnb also offers "boutique hotels," which are small, luxury hotels that provide personalized service and unique decor.

- **Shared Rooms**: For travelers looking to save money, Airbnb offers shared rooms in homes or apartments. These typically provide a shared bathroom and common areas, but with private bedrooms.

By offering these various accommodations, Airbnb makes it possible for travelers to find a comfortable and affordable place to stay, whether they're looking for a traditional vacation rental or a unique experience. Your job is to find your space according to the niche you want to serve.

The Importance of a Good Location

As a host on Airbnb,

choosing a good location for your rental property is crucial for your success.

A good site can attract more guests, increase the occupancy rate, and ultimately generate more income for you. Here are a few reasons why the location of your Airbnb is so essential:

- **Convenience**: A good location should be convenient for guests, with easy access to public transportation, local attractions, and essential amenities like grocery stores and restaurants. This can make your guests' stay more enjoyable and increase their chances of leaving a positive review.

- **Safety**: Guests want to feel safe and secure when they travel, so it's crucial to choose a location that is in a safe and secure neighborhood.

- **Attractions**: If your Airbnb is located in a popular tourist destination or near popular attractions, it can attract more guests looking to explore the area.

- **Competitive Advantage**: By choosing a good location, you can differentiate your Airbnb from others in the area and offer something unique and appealing to potential guests.

- **Higher Occupancy Rates**: A good location can help increase the occupancy rate of your Airbnb, which can translate into more income for you.

- **Repeat Business**: If your guests have a great experience staying at your Airbnb in a good location, they may be more likely to book with you again or recommend your property to their friends and family.

It's also important to consider local laws and regulations when choosing a location for your Airbnb. Make sure you are aware of any zoning laws or restrictions that may impact your ability to operate as a host in your area.

Understanding Airbnb's Value Proposition

Airbnb offers a ton of benefits to new and existing hosts. These benefits differentiate it from other similar platforms and motivate more people looking to get into the STR business to choose Airbnb as their preferred platform for hosting guests (Scarlett, 2022).

Here are some of the benefits enjoyed by Airbnb hosts:

- **Reach**: With millions of active users, Airbnb provides new and existing hosts with the ability to reach a large, global audience of potential guests. This means that even if you only have one or two listings, you can still attract many guests.

- **Flexibility**: Airbnb allows hosts to choose the dates and times they want to host guests, making it easy to fit hosting into their schedule. They can adjust their pricing and availability as needed, giving them complete control over their listings.

- **Income Generation**: Hosting guests on Airbnb can be a great way to generate additional income, whether it's to supplement a primary income source or earn a living.

With the ability to set their prices and control their availability, hosts can determine how much they make through Airbnb.

- **Community**: Airbnb has built a supportive and welcoming community of hosts and guests, providing new hosts with access to a network of experienced hosts and resources to help them succeed.

- **Trust and Safety**: Airbnb takes the safety and security of its guests and hosts seriously and provides a range of tools and resources to help ensure that both parties have a safe and enjoyable experience.

Here's a summary: Airbnb's value proposition offers hosts the ability to reach a large, global audience, generate additional income, and be part of a supportive community, all while having complete control over their listings and the ability to ensure the safety and security of their guests. By offering these unique benefits, Airbnb helps new hosts succeed as hosts and realize the full potential of hosting on its platform.

Listing a Property on Airbnb

- **Create an Airbnb account**: Go to the Airbnb website and sign up for an account as a host. Provide your personal information and payment method, and create a password.

- **List your property**: Click the "List your space" button and follow the steps to add your property. Provide the property type, address, and a brief description.

- **Set up your listing**: Add photos of your property and describe its features, amenities, and house rules. Set your desired price, availability, and minimum stay length.

- **Verify your identity**: Airbnb may ask you to verify your identity for security reasons, usually through a government-issued ID or passport.

- **Review and publish**: Review your listing and ensure everything is accurate and complete. Then click the "Publish" button to make your property available on the platform.

Tips

A good listing strategy will help you improve your chances of showing up in guest searches. Here are five ways to enhance your listing on Airbnb:

1. **Include keywords in your listing title**: Keywords are words that customers use to search for properties. It's also advisable to include your most attractive amenities in your listing title. Example: "Luxury cabin: hiking, fishing, hot tub, game room."

2. **Professional photos**: You need clear pictures and great lighting to make your property look aesthetically pleasing to prospective guests.

3. **White bedding**: This may seem funny, but crisp, hotel-standard white bedding generally makes any room look

clean and luxurious and adds to your overall aesthetic.

4. **Entertaining and relaxing features**: Having at least one relaxing feature, e.g., a hot tub or sauna, and one fun feature, e.g., a mini basketball court or video games, will attract more guests. Don't forget to include them in your listing title, description, and photos.

5. **Great background for pictures**: This is a big one. Guests love to take photos that they can post on social media. You can arrange a little space with great lighting for your guests to take pictures. This also gets you some free advertising.

The Difference Between Traditional Renting and Airbnb

Airbnb and traditional renting differ regarding rental duration and pricing, income expenses, and regulations, for example:

- **Rental duration**: Traditional renting typically requires a long-term commitment, often with a lease of 6 to 12 months. On the other hand, Airbnb offers short-term rental options, which allow travelers to rent a property for a few days or weeks. This can provide homeowners with a source of income by renting out their property while they are away.

- **Pricing (income) and expenses regulation**: The pricing of traditional rentals is usually fixed and determined by the landlord. With Airbnb, the pricing is more flexible and is generally determined by the host based on supply and demand.

- **Income and expenses**: Traditional landlords typically collect rent, which is their only source of income. On the other hand, Airbnb hosts can earn money from several sources, including rent, cleaning fees, and other services. However, Airbnb hosts are also responsible for expenses such as cleaning and maintenance, which traditional landlords typically cover.

- **Regulations**: Traditional rentals are typically subject to local housing and zoning regulations, which may dictate building and safety codes. On the other hand, Airbnb rentals can face more challenges in terms of regulation, as they operate in a gray area between personal and commercial use.

To sum it all up, Airbnb and traditional renting are two different rental options that offer distinct advantages and disadvantages. While traditional renting is more established and regulated, Airbnb provides a more flexible and potentially lucrative opportunity for renters and homeowners.

Key Takeaways

Here are the essential points from this chapter:

- Your ideal guest determines what niche of Airbnb you go into.

- The location of your Airbnb plays a significant role in the success of your business.

- Do not underestimate the power of pleasing aesthetics and professional pictures.

- Using keywords when creating your listing can help you show up more frequently during guest searches.

What Next?

- Do your research on Airbnb niches to find the area you resonate with most.

- Create your Airbnb account if you don't already have one.

- Refine your listings on Airbnb using the tips listed above.

- Practice taking aesthetically pleasing pictures in your home or an existing Airbnb.

We're moving on to the money part in the next chapter. How much can you potentially earn from Airbnb? How much does it cost to get started? Turn the page, and let's discuss how to estimate your earnings.

CHAPTER 4

Estimate Your Earnings

Revenue is vanity, profit is sanity, and cash is king.

–Alan Miltz

Making money is easy. But just how much money is it possible to make from Airbnb? In this chapter, we will explore the basics of estimating your earnings from Airbnb. The sharing economy has provided numerous opportunities for individuals to earn extra income through platforms like Airbnb. As a host, it is crucial to understand your expected earnings and the factors that can impact them. This chapter will guide you through calculating your Airbnb earnings, considering factors such as occupancy rate, nightly rate, cleaning fees, and taxes. By the end of this chapter, you will better understand what to expect from your Airbnb property and how to maximize your earnings.

Let's get started!

How Much Will You Earn?

To calculate your estimated earnings from Airbnb as a new host, you'll need to consider a few key factors:

- **Rental rate**: This is the amount you charge guests for staying on your property. To determine a competitive rental rate, you can check out similar listings in your area and see what they charge. You'll also want to consider factors like the time of year, local events, and demand for accommodations in your area, for example:

- **Occupancy rate**: This is the percentage of nights your property is rented out each month. A higher occupancy rate means more income but also higher costs for cleaning and maintenance. As a new host, it's difficult to predict your exact occupancy rate, so you can start by estimating a moderate rate (e.g., 50% occupancy).

- **Expenses**: To calculate your net income, you'll need to subtract your expenses from your rental income. Some everyday expenses include cleaning and maintenance, furnishing, property insurance, and marketing. You may also need to pay Airbnb a fee (usually around 3% of the rental income).

Example:

Let's say you're a new host and have decided to rent a one-bedroom apartment in San Francisco. After researching similar listings, you can charge $150 per night. You estimate an occupancy rate of 50% for the first year. Your expenses for cleaning and maintenance are $50 per stay, and you'll pay Airbnb a 3% fee.

Rental income: $150 x 50% = $75 per night

Expenses: $50 + ($75 x 3%) = $58.25 per night

Net income: $75 – $58.25 = $16.75 per night

So, your estimated earnings from Airbnb as a new host would be $16.75 per night. To calculate your monthly income, multiply this by the number of nights you expect to be rented each month. Remember that this is just an estimate, and your actual earnings may be higher or lower depending on various factors such as demand, competition, and expenses.

Research Your Chosen Market

Both new and existing Airbnb hosts can research their chosen market (niche) by following these steps:

1. **Location research**: Start by researching where you want to list your property. Look into the local real estate market, the tourism industry, and other factors that may impact demand for Airbnb rentals. You can use online tools such as Google Trends, Zillow, and Airbnb's search data to gather information on popular areas and price trends.

2. **Competition analysis**: Study the competition in your chosen market by searching for similar listings on Airbnb. Look at the prices, amenities, and services offered by competing listings, as well as their occupancy rates. This information will help you determine the best rental rate for your property.

3. **Market demand**: To assess demand for Airbnb rentals in your chosen market, consider factors such as the time of year, local events, and tourism patterns. You can use tools like Google Trends and Airbnb search data to see the seasonal demand for your type of property.

4. **Cost of living**: To help you determine a competitive rental rate, research the cost of living in your chosen market. Consider expenses such as property taxes, utilities, and maintenance charges when setting your rental rate.

5. **Guest preferences**: Research what guests are looking for in an Airbnb rental. Look at the reviews and ratings of similar listings and consider what features or amenities guests may value. This will help you differentiate your listing and attract more guests.

By conducting market research, new and existing Airbnb hosts can gain a deeper understanding of their chosen market and make informed decisions about their rental strategy. This can help them increase their chances of success and maximize their earnings as an Airbnb host.

Estimate Your Possible Investment

To calculate your estimated investment in a new property you want to list as an Airbnb host, you'll need to consider several vital costs, including:

- **Purchase price or rental rate**: The upfront cost of

buying or renting the property. If you are purchasing, consider additional charges such as closing fees, property taxes, and insurance.

- **Furnishing and equipment**: You may need to purchase furniture, appliances, and other items to furnish the property and prepare it for guests. Consider things such as beds, linens, kitchen supplies, and electronics.

- **Renovations and upgrades**: You may need to upgrade the property, such as with new flooring, painting, or upgrades to the bathroom or kitchen. Factor in the cost of these renovations into your estimate.

- **Marketing and advertising**: To attract guests to your property, you may need to invest in marketing and advertising. Consider expenses such as photography and video services, listing optimization, and paid advertising.

Example:

Let's say you're planning to purchase a one-bedroom apartment in New Jersey to list on Airbnb. The purchase price is $500,000. You estimate that you'll need to spend $10,000 on furniture and equipment, $5,000 on renovations and upgrades, and $1,000 on marketing and advertising.

Purchase price: $500,000

Furnishing and equipment: $10,000

Renovations and upgrades: $5,000

Marketing and advertising: $1,000

Total estimated investment: $516,000

Remember that this is just an estimate. Your actual costs may be higher or lower depending on various factors such as the property location, local taxes and regulations, and the extent of renovations required. Additionally, it's a good idea to have some extra funds set aside for unexpected expenses, such as property maintenance and repairs.

Create a Detailed Business Plan

- **Determine how much funding you will require to get started**: The first step in creating a business plan for an Airbnb host is to determine the initial funds needed. This could include the cost of purchasing or renting a property, furniture, and other necessary supplies.

- **Figure out how much your monthly recurring expenses will be**: This includes utilities, property maintenance, insurance, and any other fees that may occur every month.

- **Determine the occupancy rate required to cover monthly expenses**: Based on the monthly costs; the next step is to determine the occupancy rate required to cover these expenses. This involves estimating the number of guests you need to host and the amount they will pay to cover your costs.

- **Determine the occupancy rate required to produce a profit**: To determine the occupancy rate required to make a profit, you will need to estimate the additional revenue needed to cover your monthly expenses and generate a profit.

- **Estimate how much money you'll need to keep the business running during slow seasons**: It is vital to estimate how much you will need to keep the business running during sluggish seasons. This will help you prepare for any unexpected slow periods and ensure that you have the funds to keep your business running smoothly.

Here's a short example for the explanation above:

Suppose you have a 2-bedroom apartment in a tourist-friendly area. You have estimated that you need $20,000 for initial expenses, including rent, furniture, and supplies. Your monthly recurring payments, including utilities and property maintenance, are $1,000. To cover these expenses, you need to rent out your property for an average of 10 nights per month. To produce a profit, you want to charge $100 per night and aim to rent the property for an average of 12 nights per month. During sluggish times and slow seasons, you estimate you will need an additional $3,000 to keep the business running.

With this information, you can create a business plan that outlines your initial and monthly expenses, target occupancy rate, and estimated profit. By having a clear plan in place, you can monitor your progress and make any necessary adjustments to ensure the success of your Airbnb business.

Key Takeaways

Here are the essential lessons from this chapter:

- Market research can produce a wealth of knowledge that will aid in understanding and growing your business.

- A business plan helps you account for every eventuality that may occur in the company from the start.

- You need to be able to calculate the amount of income that will cover your expenses and produce a profit. This will help you set a target occupancy rate.

- Always set aside some money for emergencies, marketing, and advertising.

What Next?

Create a business plan for your new or current Airbnb business using the explanation above.

In Chapter 5, we'll discuss the practical steps of setting up your Airbnb. You'll also learn about some sought-after amenities to make your Airbnb awesome!

CHAPTER 5

Preparing Your Airbnb Property

The best way to find yourself is to lose yourself in the service of others.

–Mahatma Gandhi

> From first impressions to fond farewells, every aspect of your Airbnb property can shape a traveler's experience.

Are you ready to turn your space into a welcoming and memorable destination?

In this chapter, we will discuss getting your property ready to receive guests, popular and sought-after amenities, and provisions to maximize your profits. We'll also discuss property insurance for your Airbnb and managing relationships with your neighbors. If you're already a host, we'll discuss finding a missing listing.

Preparing Your Property for Airbnb

After renting a property for Airbnb or deciding to use a part of your home as an Airbnb, what next steps should you take?

1. Clean the space thoroughly, including by dusting,

vacuuming, and sanitizing surfaces.

2. Make sure all bedding and towels are fresh and laundered.

3. Stock the kitchen with basic supplies such as coffee, tea, sugar, salt, and pepper.

4. Place toiletries such as soap, shampoo, and toothpaste in the bathroom.

5. Ensure all light bulbs are working and all electrical appliances are in good condition.

6. Put fresh flowers or plants in the room for a welcoming touch.

7. Leave clear instructions for how to operate appliances, use the TV, and access Wi-Fi.

8. Provide information about local attractions, restaurants, and transportation.

9. Ensure that the property is secure with locks on doors and windows.

10. Provide guests with a map of the local area and your contact information if they need assistance during their stay.

By following these steps, you can help ensure that your Airbnb guests have a comfortable and enjoyable stay.

Increasing Your Profit Potential

Profit maximization is a critical aspect for Airbnb hosts looking to maximize their returns from their rental property. As an Airbnb host, you need to ensure that you are maximizing your profit potential by making wise financial decisions and utilizing the platform to its fullest potential. This can be achieved by understanding the opportunities that Airbnb provides and identifying areas where you can improve.

By implementing the strategies discussed in this book, you will understand how to increase your profit potential as an Airbnb host and take your earnings to the next level. Whether you're a seasoned host or just starting, this guide will provide the knowledge and tools you need to succeed in the competitive world of short-term rentals. So don't wait any longer. Keep reading to take the first step toward maximizing your profit potential!

Determining the Amenities Guests Want

This takes us back to knowing your niche. Determining the amenities guests want in an Airbnb property depends on your niche or target market. The amenities you provide can significantly impact the appeal of your property and, ultimately, your bookings and revenue. Here's how to determine the types of amenities guests want in an Airbnb based on your niche:

- **Identify your target market**: Consider who your ideal guests are and what type of experience they are looking for. For example, if you're targeting families, you may want to offer kid-friendly amenities such as toys and a pack-and-play.

- **Research your competition**: Look at similar properties in your area and see what amenities they offer. Note what sets your property apart and what amenities you can provide that your competitors do not.

- **Ask your guests**: Get feedback from your guests by sending them a survey or asking them directly during check-in or check-out. Find out what they liked and didn't like about their stay, and what amenities they would like to see in the future.

- **Offer unique amenities**: Based on your niche, consider offering unique amenities that will set your property apart from the competition. For example, if you are targeting business travelers, you may want to provide a workstation with a high-speed internet connection.

- **Consider the location**: The location of your Airbnb can also give you an idea of what amenities to add to it. If it is on a beach, you might consider stocking extra swimsuits and sunscreen. If it's a cold area, you can add some complimentary scarves, hot cocoa, etc.

Furniture and Appliances to Include for the Best Results

Here's a list of niche-based amenities that an Airbnb host can provide to increase bookings:

- **Eco-Friendly Amenities**: Offer eco-friendly products such as reusable water bottles, cloth towels, and compostable cleaning supplies.

- **Kitchen Supplies**: Stock the kitchen with basic cooking supplies, appliances, and pantry essentials to help guests cook their meals.

- **Home Office**: Provide a quiet workspace for guests who are traveling for business.

- **Fitness**: Offer a yoga mat, resistance bands, or a fitness guide for guests who enjoy working out during their travels.

- **Pet-Friendly**: Offer pet beds, bowls, and toys for guests traveling with their furry friends.

- **Local Guides**: Provide tourists with information about local attractions, restaurants, and events in the area.

- **Tech Amenities**: Offer high-speed Wi-Fi, charging ports, and a smart TV to keep guests connected and entertained.

- **Cultural Experiences**: Offer cultural activities or experiences that guests can participate in to get a taste of local life.

- **Spa & Wellness**: Offer spa amenities such as bathrobes, slippers, and essential oils to help guests relax and unwind.

- **Children's Amenities**: Provide toys, books, and games for younger guests.

By offering these unique amenities, Airbnb hosts can differentiate themselves from the competition and provide guests with an unforgettable experience.

Figuring Out a Missing Listing

Sometimes, listings disappear, which may surprise new hosts, but I'm sure experienced hosts have gone through this a couple of times. As an Airbnb host, if your listing is missing, you can follow these steps to recover it:

- **Check your account**: Log in to your Airbnb account and check if your listing is still active. If it's inactive, you may have accidentally deactivated it.

- **Contact Airbnb support**: If you can't find your listing in your account, contact Airbnb's support team for assistance. You can contact them through the Help Center or the Airbnb app.

- **Provide information**: To help Airbnb support find your missing listing, provide the name of your listing, the location, and the date it was created.

- **Check your email**: Airbnb may have sent you an email regarding any issues with your listing or account. Check your email and respond to any requests from Airbnb support.

- **Resolve any issues**: If there were any issues with your listing or account, such as policy violations or technical problems, resolve them promptly.

- **Reactivate your listing**: Once you've resolved any issues, you can reactivate your listing and make it available for booking again.

Managing Neighbors' Relations

As an Airbnb host, managing your relationship with your neighbors and resolving conflicts is crucial to ensuring a positive experience for you and your guests. Here are some tips to help you manage these relationships effectively:

- **Communicate with neighbors**: Let your neighbors know that you are hosting guests through Airbnb and keep them informed about your guests' arrival and departure times.

- **Set clear rules**: Communicate your house rules to guests and remind them to be respectful of the neighbors and keep noise levels down.

- **Address any concerns**: If your neighbors express fears, address them promptly and professionally. Listen to their point of view and find a solution that works for both parties.

- **Mediate conflicts**: In disputes between guests and neighbors, act as a mediator to resolve the issue peacefully.

- **Consider neighborhood dynamics**: Before accepting a booking, be aware of potential conflicts that may arise due to the guests' backgrounds, cultural differences, or other factors.

- **Be proactive**: Anticipate potential conflicts and take steps to prevent them from happening. For example, provide guests with earplugs if the neighbors have some construction work going on.

Follow these steps above and seek help from your homeowners' association (HOA) or law enforcement if any issues get out of hand.

Insurance for Protection

Ignoring property insurance or leaving it to the property owner (if you are a renter) can be a big mistake. Insurance is vital to protect yourself from any liabilities as a host:

- **Airbnb Host Protection Insurance**: This is insurance provided by Airbnb to its hosts, which offers liability coverage up to $1 million in the event of third-party claims of bodily injury or property damage arising from an Airbnb rental transaction. This coverage does not replace the host's homeowner's or renter's insurance.

- **Airbnb Host Guarantee**: This is a non-insurance program offered by Airbnb that provides up to $1 million in damages in the event of theft or accidental damage caused by an Airbnb guest. However, the host guarantee has some exclusions and limitations and does not cover loss of income.

- **Renters or homeowners insurance:** This type of insurance protects the personal property of the homeowner or renter as well as providing liability coverage in the event of third-party claims. Airbnb recommends that all hosts obtain a renters or homeowners insurance policy, as the coverage offered by Airbnb's host protection insurance and host guarantee is limited and may not fully protect hosts against all risks associated with renting out their property.

Be a Guest First to Better Understand Hosting

You know the guest-centered experience we keep talking about? The best way to understand it is to put yourself in the guest's shoes. Here's what I recommend: Find the most highly rated Airbnbs in your location that are associated with your niche. Book a night or two and take note of everything from the host's response to the reception on your first night. Take note of the amenities, the free stuff, the aesthetics, etc. Also, take note of how your host responds to questions and special requests.

The best way to learn what guests want is to be a guest yourself.

Key Takeaways

- Preparedness is the backbone of guest satisfaction.

- You can maintain a healthy relationship between your guests and neighbors by ensuring your neighbors are aware of the business and that guests follow your rules.

- The best way to learn what guests want is to become one yourself.

What Next?

Visit Airbnbs in your area or the location of your intended Airbnb and get a taste of the experiences other hosts have to offer.

Do you know that a good listing can determine your occupancy rate? Move to the next chapter to learn how to create the right listing for your property.

CHAPTER 6

Listing for Satisfaction

You are everywhere, but you don't have to be. Strategy is a decision to take a path, to say no.

–Kristina Halvorson

Your listing is the first contact your Airbnb has with prospective guests. So, you want to make it as enticing as possible. The success of a property on Airbnb is dependent mainly on its listing.

> A well-written and well-presented listing can help attract more guests and increase the likelihood of bookings, while a poorly executed listing may result in few or no bookings.

In this chapter, we will provide you with the essential tips and best practices for writing a compelling Airbnb listing that stands out from the competition and captures the attention of potential guests.

We will start by discussing the critical elements of a good Airbnb listing, including high-quality photos, detailed descriptions, and accurate pricing information. We will also cover how to write a compelling headline and description that highlights your property's unique features and benefits, as well as how to present your location in the best possible light.

In addition, we will discuss the importance of positive reviews and how to manage your listing's reputation, as well as how to optimize your listing for search engines to increase its visibility to potential guests. Finally, we will provide practical tips and real-life examples of successful Airbnb listings to help you put these concepts into practice and create a compelling listing that showcases your property and its unique features. Whether you are a seasoned Airbnb host or a new property owner, this chapter will provide the tools and guidance you need to write a winning Airbnb listing.

Creating an Impressive First Impression

Creating a strong first impression through your Airbnb listing can bring numerous advantages to your property and increase your chances of success. Here are some of the benefits of making a great first impression through your Airbnb listing:

- **Increased bookings**: A visually appealing and well-presented listing can attract more guests and improve your booking rate.

- **Competitive advantage**: A listing that stands out from the competition and accurately represents your property can help you differentiate yourself and attract more guests.

- **Increased trust and confidence**: Positive reviews and

clear, detailed descriptions of your property can build trust with potential guests and increase their confidence in booking your property.

- **Better reputation**: Responding promptly to negative feedback and encouraging positive reviews can help maintain a good reputation for your property and attract more bookings in the future.

By focusing on creating a solid first impression through your Airbnb listing, you can reap these benefits and increase the success of your property on the platform.

Creating a Listing That Gets Attention

Apart from high-quality photos and luxury aesthetics, the other things that can make or break your listing are your headline and description. In the following sections, we will discuss creating a good headline description. Your headline is the first thing prospective guests see, apart from the pictures you upload. You want to be as creative as possible without taking away from the actual message you are trying to convey.

A Catchy Headline

Writing a catchy headline for your Airbnb listing is crucial to catching the attention of potential guests and inspiring them to book a stay. Here are some tips to help you create a compelling headline:

- **Keep it short and sweet**: Your headline should be concise, clear, and to the point. Aim for a headline that's around 6–8 words long.

- **Use keywords wisely**: Choose words that describe your listing's unique features and selling points, such as "luxury," "oceanfront," or "romantic."

- **Be descriptive**: A headline that paints a picture of your space and the experience guests can expect will help your listing stand out. For example, "Cozy Cabin with Mountain Views and Hot Tub."

- **Make it memorable**: Use humor, puns, or wordplay to create a headline that sticks in people's minds. For example, "Escape to the Mountains—Beary Cozy Chalet."

- **Highlight location**: If your listing is popular or unique, include it in your headline. For example, "Charming Cottage in the Heart of Paris."

Examples of effective headlines:

- "Sunny Oceanfront Getaway with Private Beach Access"

- "Elegant Loft in the Heart of the City"

- "Rustic Treehouse with Hot Tub and Forest Views"

- "Luxury Apartment with Rooftop Pool and City Views"

Remember, your headline is the first thing potential guests will see, so make it count!

A Great Description

Writing a great description for your Airbnb listing is essential to attracting guests and making them want to book a stay. Here are some tips to help you create a compelling description:

- **Highlight unique features**: Focus on the things that set your space apart, such as a private hot tub, a stunning view, or stylish decor.

- **Use descriptive language**: Paint a picture of your space and the experience guests can expect. Use adjectives, sensory language, and vivid descriptions to make your listing stand out.

- **Mention the neighborhood**: Provide information about the surrounding area, such as local restaurants, attractions, and public transportation options.

- **Be specific**: Give guests all the information they need to decide, such as the number of bedrooms, bathrooms, and amenities.

- **Be honest**: Be transparent about potential challenges, such as a lack of parking or a noisy street, so that guests can make an informed decision.

Examples of great descriptions:

- "Escape to our serene mountain cabin, surrounded by lush forest and breathtaking views. Relax in the hot tub on the deck, roast marshmallows by the fire pit, or enjoy the peaceful surroundings."

- "Stay in the heart of the city in our stylish and spacious loft. With floor-to-ceiling windows and a rooftop pool, you'll enjoy breathtaking views and all the comforts of home."

- "Our cozy cottage is the perfect place to unwind and escape from the hustle and bustle of city life. With a well-appointed kitchen, comfy bed, and serene backyard, you'll feel right at home."

Setting House Rules

As an Airbnb host, setting house rules can help ensure your guests understand what is expected of them during their stay. House rules also ensure that your guests do not interfere with or infringe on the neighbors' rights and keep your property in good condition. Here's how to set House Rules:

1. Access your account and find your listing.

2. Click on the "House Rules" tab.

3. In the "House Rules" section, click on "Edit House Rules."

4. Create a list of rules you'd like your guests to follow

during their stay. Make sure to include any rules that are specific to your property, such as those about smoking, pets, or parties.

5. Be clear and concise in your language, and consider including relevant details about why the rule is in place.

6. Save your changes.

It's important to note that guests are required to agree to your house rules before they can book your listing. This can help ensure that they are aware of your expectations and can help avoid any misunderstandings during their stay. Additionally, it's a good idea to review your house rules periodically to make sure they're up-to-date and still applicable to your property.

Selecting a Cancellation Policy

Deciding on the most favorable cancellation policy can significantly impact your bookings and your income.

There are three different cancellation policies available on Airbnb, and here's a brief explanation of each one:

- **Flexible**: With this policy, guests can cancel their booking up to 48 hours before check-in and be refunded fully. This policy can appeal to guests as it offers a lot of flexibility, but it may also result in more last-minute cancellations for you as a host.

- **Moderate**: With this policy, guests can cancel their

booking up to 5 days before check-in and get their money back. This policy strikes a balance between offering some flexibility to guests and providing some protection for you as a host.

- **Strict**: With this policy, guests' payments will only be returned if their booking is cancelled within no more than 48 hours of making it. After that, no refunds will be given. This policy is best for hosts who want to reduce the risk of cancellations, but it may also make guests less likely to book your listing if they know they won't be able to get their money back if they need to cancel.

When choosing a cancellation policy, it's important to consider your preferences and the nature of your property. For example, if you have a high-demand property and are confident that you can fill any cancellations, you may be able to opt for a stricter policy. On the other hand, if your property is less in demand, you may want to offer more flexibility to guests to encourage bookings.

Appropriate and Bearable Fees

As an Airbnb host, it's important to understand the fees associated with listing your space on the platform. There are a few key fees that hosts should be aware of:

- **Service fee:** This fee is charged to guests and is a percentage of the total booking cost. It ranges from 14%

to 20% and helps cover the cost of running the Airbnb platform.

- **Cleaning fee:** This fee is optional, but it's a good idea to include it in your listing to cover the cost of cleaning after guests leave. A reasonable cleaning fee could range from $30 to $100, depending on the size of your space and the level of cleaning required.

- **Airbnb host protection fee:** This fee is optional, but it provides hosts with insurance coverage for damages caused by guests. The fee is a small percentage of the booking cost and can provide peace of mind for hosts.

It's important to keep your fees reasonable and in line with industry standards. Overcharging guests can make your listing less competitive, while charging too little could result in inadequate coverage. Remember to include these fees in your calculations.

Turning On Instant Book

As an Airbnb host, you can enable Instant Book to allow guests to book your listing without waiting for your approval. Here's how:

1. Log in to your Airbnb account and go to your listing.

2. Click on the "Calendar" tab.

3. Scroll down to the "Booking settings" section.

4. Toggle the "Instant Book" switch to the "On" position.

5. Update your listing's availability, pricing, and house rules if necessary.

6. Save your changes.

Once you have turned on Instant Book, guests can book your listing immediately if your calendar is up-to-date and it meets their needs. Make sure you review your bookings and adjust your settings as necessary to ensure that you're getting the bookings that work best for you.

Key Takeaways

- The perfect listing contains high-quality pictures, a catchy headline, and a simple but precise description.

- House rules help your guests know what is expected of them and can prevent any run-ins with neighbors.

- A reasonable cancellation policy helps minimize losses that may come from canceled bookings.

What Next?

Practice writing headlines and descriptions for your Airbnb. If you already have a few properties, refine your listing using the tips above.

Ever heard about the law of attraction? It says that you receive the energy you give out; you attract what you are. Move on to the next chapter, where we'll be learning how to attract the right kind of guests to your Airbnb.

Chapter 7

Attracting Guests

The three most important factors in attracting Airbnb guests were found to be: the overall cleanliness of the space, the accuracy of the listing description, and the quality of communication with the host.

–Hui, P. & Wang, D.

The law of attraction explains that energy is reciprocal. That means

> you have to be or look a particular way to attract certain types of people and situations.

Attracting guests to your Airbnb property can be a challenging task, especially in a highly competitive market. However, with the right strategies and techniques, you can increase your chances of attracting guests and filling up your calendar with bookings. In this chapter, we'll explore the best ways to market your Airbnb property and make it stand out from the rest.

One of the first steps to attracting guests is to have a well-presented listing. This includes high-quality photos, a detailed description of the property and its amenities, and a clear pricing structure. A good listing can make all the difference in whether a potential guest decides to book with you.

Another critical aspect of attracting guests is to provide excellent customer service. Responding promptly to inquiries and providing a welcoming and hospitable environment can create a positive impression and encourage guests to book with you again.

In addition to these basics, you can consider using various marketing techniques to increase your visibility and attract more guests. This can include using social media platforms like Instagram and Facebook to showcase your property, using paid advertising to reach a wider audience, and offering special deals and promotions to attract repeat bookings.

Professional Photography of Your Listing

Professional pictures of your Airbnb property are crucial because they play a significant role in attracting potential guests. A well-photographed listing can stand out from other similar properties and make your listing look more attractive, appealing, and trustworthy. Good photos can also help to showcase the unique features and amenities of your property and assist guests in imagining themselves staying there. Additionally, professional images can help to create an emotional connection with potential guests and increase the likelihood of bookings and repeat business. Just in case you don't have the opportunity or funds to hire a professional photographer.

Here are some tips for taking DIY, professional-looking photos of your Airbnb listing:

- **Use natural light**: Take advantage of natural light by taking photos during the day and opening curtains and blinds to let in as much light as possible. Avoid using flash photography, as it can create harsh shadows and wash out the colors of your space.

- **Consider the composition**: The "rule of thirds" is a well-known photography rule that shows people to divide the frame into three equal parts, both vertically and horizontally. This helps them make pictures that look good. The four points where these lines meet are said to be the most captivating areas of the image. If you want to show off a space on Airbnb, using the rule of thirds can make your photos more appealing:

  - For instance, when photographing a room, placing the bed or any other focal point at one of the intersecting points may result in a more engaging and interesting composition. Similarly, when capturing the exterior of the building, placing it at one of the intersecting points can produce a more balanced and eye-catching image. While there are many techniques to create spectacular images for Airbnb listings, the rule of thirds can be a useful tool to improve the quality of your pictures. It's a great starting point for those looking to fine-tune their photography skills and make their listings stand out.

- **Stage the space:** Remove clutter, tidy up, and ensure

the room looks inviting and appealing. Consider adding some simple decor elements, such as fresh flowers or a bowl of fruit, to add some visual interest.

- **Use a tripod**: A tripod can help to keep your camera steady and ensure that your photos are straight and well-composed.

- **Edit your photos**: Use basic photo-editing software to adjust the brightness, contrast, and saturation of your photos to make them look more professional.

By following these tips, you can take DIY, professional-looking photos of your Airbnb listing, that will help you attract more guests.

Photo Strategy to Attract Guests

As a host on Airbnb, the photos you upload of your property can significantly attract guests. Here's a creative photo strategy you can use:

- **Highlight the unique features of your property**: This can include a stunning view, a cozy fireplace, or a spacious outdoor area. Make sure to take photos that showcase these features and highlight why your property is different from others.

- **Showcase the space**: Take photos of each room in your property, including the living room, kitchen, bedrooms, and bathrooms. Pay attention to lighting, furniture, and décor to create a welcoming and inviting atmosphere.

- **Showcase the local area**: Take photos of local attractions, parks, and other amenities within walking distance or a short drive from your property. This will give guests an idea of what they can do in the area and what makes it unique.

- **Create a sense of lifestyle**: If your property is suitable for hosting events or gatherings, take photos that show how guests can use the space for these activities. This could include pictures of people enjoying a meal together in the kitchen, relaxing in the living room, or having a BBQ in the backyard.

It's also important to keep in mind that clear, well-lit photos are essential to making your listing look appealing. Avoid using filters or overly edited images, as this can make the space appear different than it is. Additionally, consider using a mix of wide-angle shots and close-ups to give guests a comprehensive look at your property and its features. With a thoughtful and well-executed photo strategy, you can make your Airbnb listing stand out and attract more guests.

Staging Your Property for Photos

- **Declutter**: Go room by room and remove any items that are not necessary or make the space look cluttered, such as personal items, excess furniture, or piles of clutter.

- **Clean and organize**: Make sure each room is clean, including surfaces, floors, and windows. Organize any remaining items in the room, such as books or furniture, to create a neat appearance.

- **Enhance lighting**: Use natural light or turn on lights to make sure that each room is well-lit. If necessary, consider adding lamps or other lighting fixtures to brighten up dark spaces.

- **Add finishing touches**: Consider adding decorative items, such as fresh flowers, pillows, or blankets, to create a cozy and inviting atmosphere. This will help to make your property feel like a welcoming home away from home for guests.

- **Showcase the unique features**: Make sure to highlight the unique features of your property in the photos, such as a stunning view or a cozy fireplace. Take pictures from different angles to showcase these features and make them stand out.

Getting All the Shots

Here are some additional tips for taking great pictures of your Airbnb:

- **Angles**: Shooting from a high angle can make a room appear larger, while shooting from a low angle can make it appear cozier. You can also try taking pictures of interesting architectural details, such as moldings or built-in bookshelves.

- **Edit:** Most smartphone cameras come with built-in editing tools that you can use to enhance your photos. Adjusting the brightness, contrast, and saturation can make a big difference in the final image. You can also crop your photos to remove distractions or straighten the horizon. Just be careful not to overedit, as this can make the photos look fake or unrealistic.

Working With Your Photographer to Get Great Photos

Working with a professional photographer can help you get high-quality, professional-looking photos of your Airbnb that will attract more guests and showcase your property in the best possible light. Here are some tips to help you work effectively with your photographer:

- **Communicate your vision:** Before the photo shoot, take some time to think about the look and feel you want for your photos. Do you want them to be bright and airy or moody and atmospheric? Share your vision with your photographer, so they know what you're looking for.

- **Offer a tour:** Show your photographer around the property and highlight the key features you want captured. This can include specific rooms, interesting architectural details, or outdoor spaces.

- **Take advantage of different times of day**: Different times of day can significantly impact the mood and lighting of your photos. Consider shooting at various times to get multiple images showcasing your property in different lighting conditions.

- **Review the photos**: After the photo shoot, review the photos with your photographer and provide feedback on what you like and what needs to be improved.

Identifying Tips and Tricks Used by Top Listings and Superhosts

Just in case you skipped this part, here is all the juicy information in one place and some extra:

- **Optimize your listing**: This includes high-quality photos, an accurate property description, and highlighting the unique features and amenities that guests will enjoy.

- **Quick response time**: Responding promptly to inquiries and messages from potential guests can make a big difference in securing a booking.

- **Set the right price**: Research the prices of similar listings in your area and adjust your prices accordingly. Keep in mind that setting a lower price can help you attract more bookings, but it also means you'll make less money.

- **Offer special deals and discounts**: Consider offering discounts for extended stays, last-minute bookings, or during slow seasons to attract more guests.

- **Create an accurate profile**: This includes a professional profile picture, a detailed description of your experience as a host, and positive reviews from previous guests.

- **Maintain a high rating**: Superhosts need to maintain a high rating. It is vital to keep your guests happy by providing excellent customer service, a clean and well-maintained property, and timely communication.

- **Enhance your listing with additional amenities**: Offer free Wi-Fi, a fully equipped kitchen, and access to a shared space or outdoor area.

- **Create a comfortable space**: Make sure that the bed and bedding are comfortable, the room is well-lit, and the space is clean and tidy.

- **Offer local recommendations**: Provide guests with information about the best restaurants, attractions, and shopping areas in your area.

- **Focus on guest communication**: Keep guests informed about important information, such as check-in and check-out times, parking, and any local events or attractions that may be happening during their stay.

- **Offer extra services**: Provide guests with additional services such as airport pickup, rental car service, or a private tour guide.

Key Takeaways

- Great pictures come from being intentional about angles and aesthetics.

- An excellent presentation is crucial to attracting guests.

- Be careful with editing. Too much can make your pictures look fake.

What Next?

- Find photos of Airbnbs within your niche and attempt to recreate them.

- Open social media pages for your business.

In the next chapter, you'll learn how to set your prices so that they're fair, but you're still making a decent amount of money.

CHAPTER 8

Pricing Essentials for Profit

The moment you make a mistake in pricing, you're eating into your reputation or your profits.

–Katharine Paine

Price is a crucial factor that can significantly impact consumer behavior and purchasing decisions. In a survey of over 1,000 consumers, it was found that nearly 60% of respondents considered the price to be the most critical factor when making a purchase decision (Dodds, Monroe, & Grewal, 1991).

> Pricing is a crucial aspect of any business, especially for companies operating in the sharing economy, such as Airbnb.

To achieve profitability, it is essential to understand the basics of pricing and to apply this understanding strategically and effectively.

In this chapter, we will explore the fundamental pricing principles and how they can be applied to Airbnb. We will examine the factors that can impact prices, such as supply and demand, competition, and the market. Additionally, we will look at how to set and adjust prices in response to changes in these factors. By the end of this chapter, you will have a solid understanding of the essential pricing elements and how to use this knowledge to maximize your profits on Airbnb.

Airbnb Pricing Strategy

It's time to get serious about the all-important aspect of pricing strategy. As Airbnb business owners, you understand that many factors contribute to success, but pricing can't be overlooked. A well-executed pricing strategy can be the difference between struggling to make ends meet and financial prosperity. The two essential aspects of pricing strategy are discussed below.

Determining the Baseline

As an Airbnb host, determining your baseline is a crucial step in developing a pricing strategy that maximizes your profits. The baseline is the minimum amount you need to charge for each booking to cover your costs and make a profit. It considers your expenses, such as property maintenance, utilities, insurance, cleaning fees, and other costs associated with running your Airbnb business. To determine your baseline, you should first gather information about your expenses.

You can start by creating a spreadsheet or using a financial tracking app to keep track of your costs. Then, calculate your monthly expenses, including any variable costs such as cleaning fees, and divide that by the number of nights you expect to host guests. This will give you your baseline cost per night. Once you have your baseline cost per night, you can set your prices. Of course, you don't have to charge exactly the baseline amount, in fact, it's generally a good idea to charge more. You can set prices higher during peak travel seasons, holidays, and special events and lower during slow periods. This dynamic pricing strategy allows you to adjust your prices based on demand and maximize profits.

Remember, your baseline is just a starting point, and your pricing strategy should be flexible and adaptable over time. Continuously monitor your costs and your occupancy rate, and make adjustments to your prices as needed to ensure that you're making a profit. By following these steps, you'll be well on your way to developing a pricing strategy that maximizes your earnings as an Airbnb host.

High to Low Using the Dynamic Pricing System

Dynamic pricing is a pricing strategy Airbnb owners use to adjust the price of their rental property based on real-time market demand. With the help of an algorithm, the system automatically increases or decreases the cost of a listing based on various factors, such as the occupancy rate, events in the area, and the time of year.

Here's how high-to-low dynamic pricing works for Airbnb owners:

- **High-demand periods**: During high-demand periods, such as holidays, peak travel seasons, and significant events in the area, the dynamic pricing system will automatically raise the price of the listing to reflect the increased demand. This can help Airbnb owners maximize their revenue during these periods.

- **Low demand periods**: Conversely, during low demand periods, the dynamic pricing system will automatically lower the listing price to incentivize bookings. This can help Airbnb owners fill up their calendars and minimize vacancies.

- **Real-time adjustment**: The dynamic pricing system is constantly monitoring market demand and making real-time adjustments to the listing price. The price can change multiple times a day based on the latest market data.

In conclusion, dynamic pricing helps Airbnb owners adjust their prices based on market demand, allowing them to optimize their revenue and minimize vacancies. It can be a valuable tool for managing the pricing of a rental property. Still, owners must stay informed about the factors that impact demand and periodically review their pricing strategy to ensure it aligns with their goals.

Reasons to Raise Your Prices

If you're considering increasing your rates, below are some reasons to justify your decision:

Special Events

As an Airbnb business owner, raising your prices for special events can significantly increase your revenue and take advantage of high-demand periods. Here's why and how to do it: Special events, such as holidays, music festivals, and major sporting events, often increase demand for short-term rentals. By raising your prices during these times, you can take advantage of the higher demand and earn more money for each booking.

Adjustment for Seasonality

As an Airbnb business owner, adjusting your prices for seasonality can help maximize your revenue and occupancy rate.

Seasonality refers to the fluctuation of demand for your rental property based on the time of year, such as holidays, festivals, and local events. For example, during peak tourist seasons or holidays, demand for rental properties in a specific area may increase, leading to higher prices and higher occupancy rates.

To adjust your prices for seasonality, you can also use dynamic pricing, which involves setting variable fees based on real-time supply and demand factors. Here are the steps to adjust your prices for seasonality:

1. Identify the seasonal demand patterns for your rental property by analyzing historical data on booking patterns and occupancy rates.

2. Determine the peak and low seasons for your property based on the demand patterns.

3. Set your prices accordingly for each season, taking into account the supply and demand of similar properties in the area.

4. Continuously monitor and adjust your prices based on

real-time supply and demand.

How to Raise Prices

You can use the dynamic pricing system provided by Airbnb to automatically adjust your prices based on the demand in your area. Alternatively, you can manually adjust your prices by logging into your Airbnb account and changing the nightly rate for your listing.

Reason for Discounting: First Rule

Offering discounts can effectively incentivize guests to book your Airbnb listing and help you fill any gaps in your calendar. Here are some reasons why offering discounts, particularly for more extended stays, can be a good strategy:

- **Length of Stay**: By offering a discount, you can increase the likelihood that a guest will choose your listing over others, especially if they are looking for a more extended stay. This can help you fill your calendar gaps and increase your occupancy rate.

- **Better Reviews**: When guests feel they have received good value for their money, they are more likely to leave positive reviews. Positive reviews can help boost your listing's visibility and attract future bookings.

- **Repeat Business**: Guests who have had a positive experience at your listing may be more likely to book with you again, especially if they received a discount for their stay.

- **Off-Peak Bookings**: Offering discounts for longer stays can also be an excellent way to encourage bookings during off-peak times when you may have more availability.

Thinking of All Your Expenses

The list below will help you understand and properly attend to your expenses:

- **Furnishing your Airbnb**: This could include the cost of furniture, bedding, decor items, and any labor costs associated with installing or repairing items.

- **Welcome gifts**: Offering a welcome gift to guests can help create a positive first impression and make them feel appreciated. This can be something simple like a basket of snacks or a bottle of wine, or something more elaborate like a bouquet or a custom welcome basket. The cost of welcome gifts will depend on what you choose to offer. Smaller items like snacks or a bottle of wine may only cost a few dollars, while larger or more elaborate gifts like a bouquet or a custom welcome basket could cost several hundred dollars.

- **Bills**: Depending on your Airbnb location, you may need to pay bills for utilities such as electricity, water, and internet. The cost of these bills will depend on factors like the size of your property and how frequently it is used.

- **Cleaning services**: Hiring a professional cleaning service can cost several hundred dollars per cleaning, while doing it yourself will require a time commitment and the cost of cleaning supplies.

- **Hidden structural problems**: The cost of fixing hidden structural problems will depend on the nature and extent of the issue. For example, fixing a leaky roof could cost several hundred dollars, while fixing a foundation issue could cost several thousand dollars.

- **Pricing for other services**: The cost of additional services, like airport pick-up and drop-off or the rental of different items, will depend on the specific services being provided and the location of your Airbnb. Be sure to price these services competitively and consider any costs associated with providing the service, such as fuel or rental fees.

- **Insurance**: The cost of insurance for your Airbnb listing can be affected by factors like its location and size. Liability insurance, for example, could cost several hundred dollars per year, while insurance for personal property could cost several thousand dollars per year.

Key Takeaways

- Airbnb's dynamic pricing feature can help you adjust your pricing according to the season and your choices.

- Discounts serve as incentives and can be used to encourage repeat business.

- Your expenses are a major determining factor when setting your prices.

What Next?

- Review your pricing if you are already a host on Airbnb.

- Take the list of expenses provided above and find out how much these would cost in your location or the location of your intended Airbnb.

Now that we've talked about pricing, let's go back to proper profit maximization. Turn the page to continue.

CHAPTER 9

Increasing Profit Potential

Creating value within your short-term rental property is key to enhancing your income.

–Laura Schreiber

In the world of business, profit potential is the key to success. Understanding opportunities and making wise financial decisions are crucial to increasing your profit potential and ensuring long-term success. This chapter will provide valuable insights into boosting your profit margins by exploring nontraditional listings, reducing operating costs, making the best purchases for future profits, identifying areas where you can eliminate expenses, maximizing your overall revenue potential, and creating additional revenue sources.

Whether you're a seasoned entrepreneur or just starting, these strategies will help you achieve your financial goals and succeed in the competitive business world. So, buckle up and prepare to take your profits to the next level!

Increasing Your Profit Potential

Business, as you may know, is all about making profits. Below are some profit maximization secrets:

- **Optimize your listing**: As we discussed, ensure your listing is appealing with high-quality photos and a well-written description. Highlight the unique features of your space and the amenities you provide. This helps with Search Engine Optimisation (SEO).

- **Set competitive prices**: Research comparable listings in your area to determine a fair and competitive price for your space. Consider adjusting your rates for peak travel times and special events. Do not undercharge or overcharge. Low prices do not mean more customers, and high prices do not mean fast money.

- **Enhance your guests' experience**: Providing extra amenities, such as toiletries and snacks, can help differentiate your listing and earn positive reviews from guests. I'd recommend calling ahead to ask guests what snacks they prefer.

- **Respond promptly**: Quickly respond to any inquiries or questions from potential guests to increase your chances of booking.

- **Maintain a high rating**: Encourage guests to leave positive reviews by providing a great experience. Respond to negative reviews constructively and work to resolve any issues.

- **Consider offering long-term stays**: Consider offering discounts for guests who book long-term stays, as this can increase your overall bookings and profit.

- **Utilize dynamic pricing tools**: Utilize software or tools that help you adjust your prices based on demand, seasonality, and other factors to maximize your bookings and revenue.

By following these tips, you can increase your profit potential and make your Airbnb hosting experience more successful.

Understanding Opportunities

There are several opportunities for Airbnb hosts to increase their profit potential. Here are some ways to take advantage of these opportunities:

- **Location**: List your property in a high-demand area with high tourist traffic. This will increase the chances of your property being rented out frequently.

- **Seasonality**: Be aware of peak tourist seasons and adjust your prices accordingly. During the high season, you can charge higher fees, while during the low season, you can offer discounts to attract more guests.

- **Amenities**: Offer additional amenities, such as free Wi-Fi, parking, or access to a pool, to make your property more appealing to guests.

- **Competitive Pricing**: Monitor your competition and make sure your prices are competitive. Offer discounts and promotions to attract more guests and increase bookings.

- **Guest Experience**: Provide a high-quality guest experience by ensuring your property is clean, well-maintained, and equipped with all the necessary amenities.

- **Marketing**: Use Airbnb's marketing tools to promote your property and reach a larger audience. Consider listing your property on other vacation rental websites to reach more potential guests.

Additionally, Airbnb hosts need to stay up-to-date with industry trends and changes to the platform. By keeping an eye on industry news and updates, hosts can adapt to new opportunities and stay ahead of the competition. They can also consider diversifying their rental portfolio by offering multiple properties or expanding into property sales.

Nontraditional Listings

Nontraditional listings refer to properties rented out for short-term stays through platforms like Airbnb, as opposed to traditional long-term rentals (Jang & Lee, 2019). In simpler terms, "nontraditional" listings refer to properties that are not traditional homes or apartments but rather unique or unusual spaces available for short-term rental. These include treehouses, yurts, houseboats, RVs, tents, and other alternative accommodation options. These types of listings can provide travelers with an experience that is different from the traditional hotel or resort stay and can offer a unique and memorable vacation experience. By providing these listings, Airbnb has expanded its market and appealed to a broader range of travelers looking for different travel experiences.

Reducing Operating Costs: Spending Smart

Cutting costs is a great way to save cash and divert your funds to other productive things. Airbnb hosts can reduce their operating costs in several ways:

- **Energy efficiency**: Hosts can invest in energy-efficient appliances, lighting, and other products to reduce their energy bills.

- **Furnishings**: Hosts can choose cost-effective and durable furniture and household items that will last a long time and reduce the need for frequent replacements.

- **Linens and towels**: Hosts can opt for bulk purchases of linens and towels to reduce the cost per unit and lower the overall cost of supplies.

- **Cleaning**: Hosts can handle cleaning and maintenance tasks themselves or hire a cleaning service at a reduced rate by opting for a less frequent cleaning schedule.

- **Maintenance**: Regular property maintenance can help reduce the need for significant repairs in the future and keep the property in good condition for guests.

- **Marketing**: Hosts can reduce the cost of marketing by utilizing social media, word-of-mouth referrals, and other low-cost marketing methods.

- **Tax deductions**: Hosts can take advantage of tax deductions available for short-term rentals, such as deductions for mortgage interest, property taxes, and depreciation.

The Best Purchases That You Can Make Now for Future Profits

This section is for emphasis. Just because you are trying to spend wisely doesn't mean you should skimp on certain things. As an Airbnb host, you can make several purchases that can help you increase your future profits:

- **Energy-efficient appliances**: Investing in energy-efficient appliances such as refrigerators, air conditioners, and lighting can help lower your energy bills and make your property more appealing to guests.

- **Durable furnishings**: Choose durable, comfortable, and aesthetically pleasing furnishings, as these can help create a positive experience for guests and reduce the need for frequent replacements.

- **High-quality linens and towels**: Investing in high-quality linens and towels can provide guests with a more luxurious experience and reduce the cost per unit in the long run.

- **Smart home technology**: Installing innovative home technology such as smart locks, thermostats, and lighting systems can make your property more convenient for guests and easier to manage remotely.

- **Professional cleaning equipment**: Purchasing professional cleaning equipment and supplies can help maintain the property to a high standard without hiring a cleaning service.

- **Marketing materials**: Investing in marketing materials such as professional photography and high-quality descriptions can help you stand out from the competition and attract more guests to your property.

Identifying What You Can Eliminate

Outsourcing is vital for productivity in any business. As an Airbnb host, you can outsource various tasks to reduce your workload and increase efficiency. Here are some examples of jobs you can outsource and how to do so:

- **Cleaning**: You can hire a cleaning service to handle the cleaning and maintenance of your property between guests. You can search for local cleaning companies or individuals who offer these services and negotiate a contract that works for both parties.

- **Key exchange**: You can use a key exchange service to handle the check-in and check-out processes for your guests. This service can provide guests with a key or code to access the property and can handle any communication and coordination required.

- **Maintenance**: You can hire a handyperson or contractor to handle maintenance tasks, such as repairing faucets or fixing a damaged wall. You can search for local services and negotiate a contract for regular maintenance.

- **Marketing and advertising**: You can hire a marketing professional or agency to handle your property's marketing and advertising efforts. This can include creating and managing your listings, taking advantage of social media marketing, and developing targeted advertising campaigns.

- **Bookkeeping and accounting**: You can outsource your bookkeeping and accounting tasks to a professional accountant who can handle your financial reporting, tax preparation, and other tasks.

By outsourcing these tasks, you can focus on the aspects of your Airbnb business that you enjoy and excel at while freeing up your time to handle other duties or responsibilities.

Maximizing Overall Revenue Potential

Maximize your revenue potential by pricing your property

competitively, maintaining a high standard of cleanliness, investing in quality furnishings, utilizing effective marketing strategies, offering flexible check-in and check-out times, and adding additional amenities such as Wi-Fi, cable TV, and self-serve breakfast items. A clean and well-maintained property with comfortable furnishings, professional photography, and well-written descriptions can help attract positive reviews and repeat bookings. Offering additional amenities can increase your property's appeal and make it stand out.

Creating Additional Revenue Sources

As an Airbnb host, you can create additional revenue streams by diversifying your offerings and tapping into new markets. Here are some ways to do so:

- **Provide more value**: You can offer other services, such as airport transportation, grocery delivery, or in-room massage services, to guests.

- **Rent out your property for events**: You can rent out your property for events such as photo shoots, weddings, or corporate events.

- **Rent out storage space**: If you have extra space on your property, you can rent it out as storage space to individuals or businesses.

- **Rent out your property for long-term stays**: You can rent out your property for long-term stays, such as a month or more, to travelers or business professionals.

- **Rent out your property to film crews**: You can rent out your property to film crews for use as a location for film or photography shoots.

It's important to carefully consider the local regulations and any additional expenses involved in offering these services, as well as the level of effort required to manage them.

Key Takeaways

Here are the top points from this chapter:

- Your listing, the experience you provide, and your pricing are the keyways to optimize your listing.

- Spend wisely, but don't cut corners. Spend if it will save you time or energy that can be put into more productive work.

- Do not be afraid to diversify.

What Next?

- Create a budget for your business—create a list of long-term investments, a list of tasks you can outsource and their costs, and a list of ways you can reduce operational costs.

- Look at the list of additional income sources and note the ones you can start.

We've talked a lot about profits, but you must be careful not to set prices that drive potential guests away. In the next chapter, we learn to choose sanity over profits, so turn the page to get started.

CHAPTER 10

Sanity Over Profits

Price is what you pay. Value is what you get.

–Warren Buffett

In the case of Airbnb, the value to the guest lies in the quality of the experience and the feeling of comfort and home they get while staying there. High prices might not necessarily equate to better value. A reasonable price point can lead to higher occupancy rates, repeat business, and positive reviews—all crucial factors in building a successful Airbnb business. In this chapter, we will explore the concept of responsible hosting and what it means to be a "superhost." We will delve into the requirements for achieving Superhost status as well as tips for maintaining this distinction.

Moreover, we will also explore different ways to streamline your hosting business through automation and outsourcing, allowing you to focus on the most crucial aspect of your business—providing a memorable and enjoyable experience for your guests. By balancing the pursuit of profits with the need for a sane and fulfilling life, you can build a successful and sustainable Airbnb business.

Choosing Sanity Over Profits

In the context of Airbnb hosting, this means setting reasonable and sustainable prices rather than pushing for the highest possible earnings. This approach considers the market conditions and the needs of both the host and the guests to create a mutually beneficial experience. Hosts who choose sanity in pricing over profits are more likely to attract a steady stream of guests.

> It's essential to strike a balance between making a profit and providing a reasonable value to guests.

By setting prices that align with market conditions, hosts can ensure that their guests have a positive experience, which will lead to repeat business and positive reviews. On the other hand, overpricing or undervaluing your property can lead to low occupancy rates and negative reviews, which can hurt your business in the long run. So, finding the right balance between sanity and profitability is vital to success in the Airbnb hosting business.

How to Host Responsibly

Responsible hosting, defined as a hosting behavior that balances the interests of the hosts, guests, and communities where the hosting activities occur, is crucial for the sustainability and success of the sharing economy (Kim & Kim, 2020). Hosting an Airbnb property responsibly involves taking some steps to ensure the safety and comfort of your guests while also respecting the rules and regulations of your local community.

Here are some tips to help you host responsibly:

- **Provide accurate descriptions and photos**: Ensure your listing accurately reflects the property and its amenities. Provide clear, detailed reports and high-quality images to give guests a clear idea of what to expect when they arrive.

- **Comply with local laws and regulations**: Familiarize yourself with the laws and regulations that apply to Airbnb hosting in your area. Make sure that you have obtained any necessary licenses or permits, and follow all rules related to zoning, safety, and taxes.

- **Maintain a clean and well-maintained property**: Keep your property clean and well-maintained. Provide clean bed linens and towels, and ensure all appliances and fixtures are in good working order.

- **Communicate with guests**: Respond promptly to inquiries and provide clear and concise information about your property and its features. Be available to answer questions or provide assistance during their stay.

- **Respect the privacy of your guests**: Ensure that guests have a quiet and peaceful stay. Avoid disturbing them during their visit, and respect their privacy by giving them space and allowing them to enjoy their time at your property.

- **Follow proper check-in and check-out procedures**: Provide clear instructions for checking in and out, and be available to assist guests if they need help. Make sure that the property is secure and that all personal belongings have been removed after a guest has checked out.

What Makes a Superhost?

Have you heard the saying, "Not all superheroes wear capes?" There are superheroes in the Airbnb business as well; they are called "Superhosts." A Superhost on Airbnb is a host who has consistently provided a high level of hospitality to their guests. Superhost status is awarded to hosts who have consistently demonstrated a commitment to providing a positive and memorable experience for their guests. Being a Superhost can lead to increased visibility on Airbnb and can help a host attract more guests and generate more bookings.

Superhost Requirements

To become a Superhost, a host must meet several criteria, including:

- **High levels of hosting Activity**: Superhosts must have hosted a certain number of trips and have a high overall booking rate.

- **Positive Guest Reviews**: Superhosts must have

received a high average rating from their guests and have a high percentage of positive reviews.

- **Low Cancellation Rates**: Superhosts must have a low cancellation rate, indicating they are reliable and responsible.

- **No Recent Policy Violations**: Superhosts must comply with Airbnb's policies and guidelines and must not have any recent policy violations.

- **Good Response Time**: Superhosts must respond promptly to guests' inquiries and messages, indicating they are available and eager to provide a high level of hospitality.

How to Maintain Superhost Status

To maintain Superhost status on Airbnb, hosts must continue to provide a high level of hospitality and meet the criteria set by Airbnb. Here are some tips to help you maintain your Superhost status:

- **Provide excellent service**: Continuously strive to provide an exceptional experience for your guests and address any issues or concerns promptly and professionally.

- **Respond quickly to guest inquiries**: Respond to guest inquiries and messages promptly, and be available to answer questions or provide assistance during their stay.

- **Maintain a clean and well-maintained property**: Keep your property clean and well-maintained, and address any maintenance issues promptly.

- **Stay compliant with Airbnb's policies**: Familiarize yourself with Airbnb's policies and guidelines, and make sure that you comply with all of them.

- **Seek feedback from guests**: Ask guests for feedback after their stay, and use their feedback to improve your listing and service.

- **Continuously improve your listing**: Regularly update your listing description, photos, and amenities to keep it fresh and appealing to guests.

By following these tips, you can maintain your Superhost status and continue to provide a high level of hospitality to your guests. Maintaining your Superhost status can help you attract more guests, earn positive reviews, and increase your bookings on Airbnb.

Automating to Make Your Life Easier

According to Liu and Wang (2021), "Automation can significantly improve the efficiency and profitability of Airbnb hosting by streamlining various tasks, such as setting prices, managing reservations, and communicating with guests."

As an Airbnb host, automating processes and outsourcing tasks can help you save time and make your life easier.

Here are some ways you can do this:

- **Hire a good manager**: Hiring a professional property manager can help you manage your Airbnb property more efficiently. They can handle tasks such as cleaning, maintenance, and guest communication, freeing up your time to focus on other things.

- **Outsource cleaning and maintenance**: Hiring a cleaning and maintenance service can help you keep your property in top condition without spending much time and effort on it. You can also outsource tasks such as laundry and linen service.

- **Use Airbnb's automation tools**: Airbnb offers a range of automation tools to help you streamline your listing and communication with guests. For example, you can set up automatic pricing and booking rules and use pre-written messages to respond to guests' inquiries.

- **Automate your billing and payment process**: You can use tools like PayPal or Stripe to automate your billing and payment process. This can help you manage time and mitigate the risk of manual errors.

- **Use scheduling software**: You can use scheduling software such as Calendly to automate your booking and check-in processes. This can help you reduce your time spent answering guest inquiries and scheduling appointments.

By automating processes and outsourcing tasks, you can reduce the time and effort you spend managing your Airbnb property, freeing up more time for yourself. Hiring a good manager can help you manage the day-to-day operations more efficiently and ensure your guests have a positive experience.

Key Takeaways

- Unreasonable prices drive guests away, even if you feel like you are providing good value for the money.

- It's not enough to become a super host. You must maintain the status.

- Automate and outsource between your means to ensure your business is moving at optimum productivity.

What Next?

- Learn how to use Airbnb's automation tools.

- Make a list of tasks you can outsource for a reasonable price.

Want to learn the secrets to the ultimate guest experience? Turn the page!

CHAPTER 11

Mastering the Guest Experience

Hospitality is an industry. It is also how we treat each other—in our own industries, communities and families.

–Danny Meyer

From the moment a guest walks through your doors to the moment they leave, every interaction and detail counts. According to the Journal of Hospitality and Tourism Research (2012), a positive guest experience boosts guest satisfaction, increasing guest loyalty and positive word-of-mouth referrals. The guest experience is the make-or-break factor for any business in the hospitality industry. Mastering the guest experience is the key to creating loyal customers and building a thriving business. But where do you start? In this chapter, we dive into the secrets of creating a world-class guest experience that will have your guests raving about their stay for years.

Understanding Being a Genuinely Good Host

Being a genuinely good host is a combination of hospitality and warmth, coupled with a genuine desire to make your guests feel comfortable and valued. Whether you're a professional in the hospitality industry or hosting guests in your home, creating a positive guest experience is a crucial factor in building lasting relationships and positive word-of-mouth referrals.

At its core, being a good host is about understanding your guests' needs and providing them with a personalized experience. This starts with simple things like greeting them with a smile, making sure they have everything they need to feel comfortable, and taking the time to get to know them. It also means anticipating their needs and providing thoughtful touches that make their stay memorable. This could be anything from a warm welcome note in their room to a small token of appreciation at the end of their stay.

To be a genuinely good host, it's crucial to create an atmosphere of warmth and comfort. This means paying attention to the little details, such as ensuring your guests have a comfortable place to sleep, providing them with clean and fresh linens, and making sure they have access to all the amenities they need. It also means going the extra mile to ensure they feel at home, such as offering a hot cup of tea or coffee in the morning or providing a simple but delicious breakfast.

One of the most important aspects of being a good host is being a good listener. This means taking the time to understand your guests' needs and preferences and responding to them promptly and thoughtfully. For example, if a guest mentions they have a food allergy, take the time to accommodate their needs and provide them with alternative options.

Another critical aspect of being a good host is ensuring your guests feel safe and secure. This means taking steps to ensure the safety of your guests, such as providing them with secure locks on their doors or ensuring that their personal information is protected. It also means making sure your guests feel physically safe, such as by providing adequate lighting or taking steps to prevent slip-and-fall accidents.

Finally, being a genuinely good host is about creating a memorable experience that your guests will want to share with others. This could be as simple as providing them with a local area map or offering suggestions for local attractions and restaurants. Or, it could be more elaborate, such as organizing a special event or activity for your guests to enjoy.

> A good host creates a warm, comfortable, and memorable guest experience.

It's about understanding their needs and preferences, making them feel safe and secure, and going the extra mile to make their stay unforgettable. Whether you're a professional in the hospitality industry or just hosting guests in your home, taking the time to be a good host will help you build lasting relationships and a positive reputation.

Understanding the Guest Search Experience

As an Airbnb host, understanding the guest search experience is vital to attracting the right guests and providing them with a positive stay. The guest search experience on Airbnb is a crucial factor in determining the success of a listing, as it heavily influences the likelihood of a reservation being made (Johnson & Smith, 2019). The guest search experience refers to the journey that guests take from the moment they start looking for a place to stay to the moment they book.

The first step in understanding the guest search experience is to understand what guests are looking for. This includes things like location, price, and amenities. Ensure your listing is accurate and up-to-date, highlighting the key features of your property and the local area.

Another critical aspect of the guest search experience is the presentation of your listing. Like we said before, make sure your photos are clear and high-quality and show off the best features of your property. Be sure to include clear descriptions of the space and any amenities, and consider including a virtual tour to give guests a better sense of the room.

In addition to the visual elements, consider the guest's experience when booking a stay. Ensure your booking process is clear and straightforward, and respond to guests quickly and professionally to ensure a smooth booking experience.

Finally, be aware of your reputation and the reviews left by past guests. Positive reviews can be a valuable tool in attracting new guests, while negative reviews can be a warning sign of issues with your property or hosting style. Encourage guests to leave reviews and consider their feedback when changing your property or hosting style.

Identifying the Fundamentals of Guest Satisfaction

Guest satisfaction is a crucial factor in the success of any hospitality business, as it determines whether guests will return and recommend the company to others. Several fundamentals of guest satisfaction should be considered to ensure a positive guest experience.

- **Cleanliness**: Ensure your property is cleaned to a high standard, paying attention to details such as fresh linens, clean bathrooms, and spotless floors.

- **Comfort**: Comfort is a significant factor in guest satisfaction. Ensure your property has comfortable beds, ample lighting, and good air conditioning and heating.

- **Convenience**: Guests expect their stay to be convenient and hassle-free. This includes easy check-in and check-out, ample parking, access to Wi-Fi, dining options, and entertainment.

- **Customer Service**: Ensure your staff is trained to provide a high level of service and is equipped to handle guests' needs and requests.

- **Personalization**: Personalization can help guests feel valued and appreciated, leading to higher satisfaction levels. Consider ways to personalize guests' experiences, such as by offering a warm welcome, providing a personal touch in their room, or offering recommendations for local attractions and dining options.

- **Value**: Guests want to feel like they are getting value for their money. Offer competitive pricing and provide guests with clear information about the amenities and services included in their stay.

Guest-Centric Plan

The guest-centric approach to hospitality has been shown to lead to higher levels of guest satisfaction and loyalty, as well as increased revenue for the property (Johnson, 2019). A guest-centric plan is a comprehensive approach to hospitality that prioritizes the guest experience. It involves putting guests at the center of all operations and deciding based on what will provide them with the best possible experience.

The guest-centric plan is centered on the following:

- **Warming check-in process**: A warm check-in process sets the tone for the entire stay by making guests feel welcomed and appreciated when they arrive. This can include offering a warm greeting, providing guests with information about the property, and helping them with their bags.

- **Communicating check-in information with guests**: Communication is critical to a positive guest experience, especially during check-in. Make sure to share all relevant information with guests, such as check-in times, parking arrangements, and access to amenities.

- **Continuing a stress-free guest stay**: A stress-free stay is essential for guest satisfaction. Ensure that guests have everything they need to feel comfortable and relaxed throughout their stay, including access to amenities, a clean and comfortable room, and prompt service when they need it.

- **Catering to your ideal guest type**: Understanding your ideal guest type means understanding your guests and what they are looking for in a stay.

- **Check-in to check-out**: The guest experience should be seamless from check-in to check-out. Ensure guests have everything they need throughout their stay and that the check-out process is smooth and stress-free.

- **Ensuring your guests enjoy their arrival**: A positive arrival experience is essential for setting the tone for the rest of the stay. Consider ways to make guests' arrivals special and memorable, such as by offering a welcome drink, providing a tour of the property, or offering a special treat in their room.

- **Setting the tone for your guests stay**: This is important for creating a positive and welcoming atmosphere. Consider things like ambient lighting, background music, and the overall décor of the property.

- **Ensuring a smooth check-out**: A smooth check-out process is an essential part of a positive guest experience. Ensure guests have all the information they need for a stress-free check-out, such as how to return keys or when to vacate their room.

According to Nyuyen and Tran (2020), "The guest-centric planning approach, which prioritizes the needs and preferences of guests in the design and management of Airbnb listings, has been shown to significantly improve the performance of these listings in terms of both occupancy rates and guest ratings."

What to Do After Guests Leave

After guests leave your Airbnb, there are several steps you can take to ensure a smooth and efficient transition. Here are some tips:

- **Clean and restock the property**: Clean the property and restock any supplies that were used during the guest's stay. This will prepare the space for the next guests.

- **Collect and wash linens**: Collect and wash all used linens to ensure they are fresh and ready for the next guests.

- **Respond to reviews**: Respond to any reviews left by guests and consider any constructive feedback when making changes or improvements to your Airbnb.

- **Check for damage**: Inspect the property for any damage or wear and tear and make necessary repairs.

- **Update your listing**: Update your Airbnb listing with any changes or updates, such as new photos or information about the property.

- **Reach out to your guests**: Consider reaching out to them after they have left to thank them for their stay and ask for any feedback on their experience.

- **Review financials**: Ensure that all payments have been processed correctly and that you have received your earnings from the total number of days the guest(s) stayed.

Managing and Responding to Guest Reviews

As an Airbnb host, managing and responding to guest reviews is an essential part of providing a positive experience for your guests and maintaining a solid reputation on the platform. Here are some tips for effectively managing and responding to guest reviews:

- **Respond promptly**: Respond to reviews as soon as possible, especially if the guest has left a negative review. This shows that you are responsive and care about the guest's experience.

- **Be polite and professional**: Regardless of the nature of the review, maintain a courteous and professional tone in your response. Avoid becoming defensive or engaging in any arguments. Thank the guest for their feedback and acknowledge any concerns they may have raised.

- **Offer solutions**: If the guest has raised a specific issue, offer solutions or steps you have taken to address the problem.

- **Take action**: Use guest reviews as an opportunity to improve your Airbnb. Consider any constructive feedback and make changes to enhance the guest experience.

Remember that reviews are an opportunity to learn and grow as a host. Stay positive and focused on providing the best possible experience for your guests.

Key Takeaways

Here are the key points from this chapter:

- The guest-centric plan is the best approach to ensuring guest satisfaction.

- Guest satisfaction is based on the experience you provide.

- Use constructive criticism from guest reviews to improve your presentation and customer experience.

- A seamless check-in/check-out process can encourage repeat business.

What Next?

- Go through the reviews of popular Airbnbs in your niche. Read them and note how the host responded.

- Use the guest-centric plan and the fundamentals of guest satisfaction to create a custom guest experience plan for your current or future guests.

Learn how to use your creativity to attract guests in the next chapter!

CHAPTER 12

Unique Airbnb Concepts

Airbnb is about belonging anywhere. The idea is to create a world where anyone can belong anywhere.

–Brian Chesky

Airbnb offers a unique opportunity to not only travel the world but also to be a part of someone else's home and story while sharing your own with the world. With co-hosting, Airbnb has revolutionized the way we travel, allowing hosts to not only monetize their spaces but also build relationships and connect with travelers from all over the globe. This chapter will focus on co-hosting, an essential aspect of Airbnb that allows you to manage other people's listings, scale your income, and explore new markets. We will also look at how to determine when to subdivide your Airbnb, add an accessory dwelling unit, host without property, and host an experience.

Finally, we will cover the keys to successful experiences and provide some ideas for brainstorming unique Airbnb experience concepts. Whether you are a seasoned Airbnb host or just starting, this chapter will provide the tools and insights you need to take your Airbnb business to the next level.

Airbnb Co-Hosting

Airbnb co-hosting refers to sharing the responsibilities of hosting an Airbnb property with another person. Co-hosting, or the use of multiple hosts to manage a single Airbnb listing, has been shown to improve the overall performance of the listing in terms of occupancy rates, guest ratings, and revenue generation (Zhang & Chen, 2021). This means that one person, the primary host, will handle the majority of the day-to-day tasks associated with hosting an Airbnb property, such as communication with guests, cleaning, and managing bookings. At the same time, the co-host provides support and assistance as needed.

For example, Sarah owns a vacation rental property in the mountains, but she lives in the city and can't manage the property daily. She can enlist the help of a resident named John to be her co-host. John can handle tasks such as greeting guests, handling check-in and check-out procedures, and managing any issues that may arise during a guest's stay. In return, John will receive a portion of the rental income generated by the property. This allows Sarah to monetize her property without being physically present, and it also provides John with a source of additional income. In this way, Airbnb co-hosting is a win-win situation for both parties, allowing them to share the responsibilities and benefits of hosting an Airbnb property.

Co-hosting is different from property management, however. A manager is employed by an Airbnb host to manage the property and assign tasks. A manager receives a salary, not a portion of the earnings.

What It Takes to Manage Other People's Listings

Managing other people's listings as a co-host on Airbnb requires a combination of technical and interpersonal skills. Here are some of the critical responsibilities and tasks involved in managing other people's listings:

- **Communication**: Good communication ensures a smooth and successful guest experience. As a co-host, you will be responsible for responding to guests' questions and inquiries, handling any issues during a guest's stay, and communicating with the primary host as needed.

- **Cleaning and maintenance**: Ensuring the property is clean and well-maintained is crucial for maintaining high ratings and attracting repeat business. As a co-host, you may be responsible for cleaning the property before and after each guest's stay, as well as performing routine maintenance tasks.

- **Booking management**: You must be familiar with the Airbnb platform and be able to manage the property's calendar and bookings. This may include accepting or declining booking requests, adjusting prices and availability, and handling cancellations and refunds.

- **Guest experience**: Your goal as a co-host is to ensure guests have a positive and memorable experience during their stay. This may include recommending local attractions and activities, resolving issues during a guest's stay, and ensuring the property is well-stocked and equipped with amenities.

- **Financial management**: As a co-host, you may be responsible for collecting payments from guests, paying bills related to the property, and keeping track of the property's income and expenses.

To be successful as a co-host, you will need to be organized, detail-oriented, and able to handle multiple tasks and responsibilities. You must also work well with others, have good interpersonal skills, and communicate comfortably with guests. Additionally, you should have a good understanding of the Airbnb platform and be familiar with the local market and regulations.

Scaling Your Income Through Co-Hosting

Scaling your income through co-hosting on Airbnb requires strategic planning and effort. Here are some tips for scaling your income as a co-host:

- **Take on multiple properties**: The more properties you manage, the more potential income you can earn as a co-host. By taking on numerous properties, you can increase your earning potential and diversify your income streams.

- **Optimize pricing**: As a co-host, you can help the primary host optimize pricing for their listings to maximize occupancy and revenue. This may involve conducting market research, adjusting prices based on demand, and using dynamic pricing tools.

- **Provide more services**: You can also increase your earnings by offering other services to guests, such as airport transportation, meal delivery, or local tours. By providing these additional services, you can generate extra revenue and provide added value to guests.

- **Build your reputation**: Building a positive reputation as a co-host is essential for scaling your income. By consistently delivering high-quality guest experiences and earning positive reviews, you can attract more guests and increase your earning potential.

- **Network with other hosts**: Networking with other hosts in your area can help you identify new opportunities for co-hosting and expanding your income streams. By building relationships with other hosts, you can access their properties, increase your visibility on the Airbnb platform, and attract new guests.

Scaling your income through co-hosting requires effort, dedication, and a willingness to improve and grow your business continuously. By following these tips and building a solid reputation as a reliable and professional co-host, you can increase your earning potential and develop your Airbnb business.

Dive Into Subdivisions of Economics

Within Airbnb, there are several subdivisions or product offerings that cater to different types of travelers and their needs. These include:

- **Airbnb Homes**: This is the traditional home-sharing product that allows individuals to rent out a room, a house, or an apartment to travelers.

- **Airbnb Experiences**: This product offers unique experiences led by local hosts, such as cooking classes, guided tours, and outdoor adventures.

- **Airbnb Adventures**: This new product offering provides multi-day trips and camping excursions with a local host.

- **Airbnb Luxe**: This premium home-sharing product offers high-end properties and villas for travelers seeking luxury accommodations.

- **Airbnb for Work**: This product is designed for business travelers and provides a range of work-friendly spaces, from private rooms to shared offices.

Determining When to Subdivide Your Airbnb

The decision on which Airbnb subdivision to enter depends on several factors, including your interests, resources, and goals. Below are some factors laid out for your consideration:

- **Property type**: If you have a unique property, such as a treehouse or a yacht, you may want to consider Airbnb Adventures or Airbnb Luxe. If you have a traditional home or apartment, you could consider Airbnb homes.

- **Hosting skills**: If you have expertise in or passion for a specific activity, such as cooking or hiking, you may want to consider Airbnb Experiences. If you have strong organizational and management skills, you may want to consider becoming a co-host for an existing Airbnb listing.

- **Target audience**: Consider your target audience and what they are looking for. For example, if you have a luxurious property, you may want to target high-end travelers through Airbnb Luxe. If you have a home close to a popular tourist destination, you may wish to target travelers looking for a comfortable and affordable place to stay through Airbnb Homes.

- **Resources**: Consider your resources, such as time, money, and energy. Some Airbnb subdivisions, such as Airbnb Adventures, may require more upfront investment and resources, while others, such as Airbnb Homes, may require a more hands-on approach in terms of property maintenance and guest communication.

Adding an Accessory Dwelling Unit

An Accessory Dwelling Unit (ADU) is a small, separate living space added to an existing property. ADUs are sometimes referred to as "granny flats," "in-law units," or "secondary units" and can be listed as properties on Airbnb. Some common types of ADUs include:

- **Detached ADUs**: A standalone structure on the same property as the main dwelling, such as a converted garage or a new building.

- **Attached ADUs**: An addition to the main dwelling, such as a converted basement, attic, or garage.

- **Internal ADUs**: A portion of the main dwelling converted into a separate living space, such as a converted bedroom or a partitioned area.

ADUs are a great option if you don't want to get a separate property or want to expand. However, there are things you must do before adding an ADU to an existing property, which includes:

- **Check local regulations**: Before you build or convert a space into an ADU, you must check your local zoning laws and regulations. Some cities have specific guidelines for ADUs and may have restrictions on their use, size, and location.

- **Obtain necessary permits**: Once you have determined that your local regulations allow for ADUs, you must obtain any required permits and approvals from your local government. This may include building permits, electrical permits, plumbing permits, and more.

Hosting Without a Property

Becoming an Airbnb host without owning property can be done by renting a place and getting the owner's permission to list it on the platform. Here are the steps you can follow:

1. **Find a place to rent**: Look for a place that meets Airbnb's requirements for safety, comfort, and cleanliness.

2. **Get the owner's permission**: Contact the property owner and ask permission to list the space on Airbnb. Make sure this is captured in writing.

3. **Set up your listing**: Once you have the owner's permission, sign up for an Airbnb account and create a listing for the space. Ensure to provide accurate and detailed information about the space, including photos and a description.

Here's a strategy for convincing landlords from James Zachary Murphy. Note that you can only use this if you're in it for the long haul.

- **Guarantee them 3 to 5 years of monthly rent**: Landlords usually get an average of 1 vacancy per year.

With your offer, they would be sure of gaining 3–5 years of constant rent.

- **Guarantee that you will keep the property in excellent condition**: One primary reason some landlords wouldn't want an Airbnb business on their property is because of damages. If you assure them that you will keep up with the cleaning and maintenance of the property, they are sure to be convinced.

- **Offer to take care of minor repairs**: Taking care of small repairs like a broken window or a leaky faucet is also a great addition to your proposal.

Be ready to sign a separate agreement for all this, though. Having it in writing will boost the landlord's confidence in you.

Hosting an Experience

As an Airbnb host, you can offer your guests more than just a place to stay. By hosting an experience, you can provide them with a unique and memorable trip that will leave a lasting impression.

> Whether you're passionate about food, art, or nature, hosting can be a fun way to connect with guests and share your passions.

Tips for hosting an experience:

- **Choose a theme that aligns with your interests and skills**: For example, if you're an experienced cook, you could host a cooking class showcasing local cuisine.

- **Be creative and think outside the box**: Offer something guests won't be able to find anywhere else, such as a guided hike to a hidden waterfall or an exclusive tour of a local art gallery.

- **Make it interactive and hands-on**: Encourage guests to participate and get involved in the experience rather than just observing.

- **Plan and be well-prepared**: Make sure you have all the necessary materials, equipment and supplies, and be prepared to handle any unexpected situations that may arise.

- **Be passionate and enthusiastic**: Your energy and excitement will be contagious and will make the experience even more memorable for your guests.

Examples of experiences:

- **Food and drink**: Offer a food tour of your local neighborhood, a cooking class, or a wine and cheese tasting.

- **Adventure and nature**: Lead a guided hike, a kayaking trip, or a surf lesson.

- **Art and culture**: Give a tour of local museums and galleries, a workshop on traditional crafts, or a concert in an intimate setting.

Understanding the Keys to Successful Experiences

Here are three critical elements for a successful experience as an Airbnb host:

- **Relevance**: Choose an experience relevant to your guests' interests and needs. Offer something unique and memorable that they can't find anywhere else.

- **Preparation**: Plan and be well-prepared. Make sure you have all the necessary materials, equipment, and supplies, and are prepared to handle any unexpected situations that may arise.

- **Flexibility**: Be flexible and open to feedback from guests. Be willing to adapt and make changes based on their suggestions and preferences.

Brainstorming a Unique Airbnb Experience Concept

Here's a process I would follow if I were looking to provide a unique experience. After identifying your niche, you should look for interests associated with that particular group. Next, you want to look for opportunities or experiences that other hosts are currently providing that are in line with those interests. Also, look for market gaps, that is, opportunities (legal) that are in demand but are not being offered. Finally, incorporate these opportunities into your own guest experience.

Here's an example:

Niche: Sustainability and Eco-Living:

Title: Off-Grid Eco-Adventure: Live Like a Homesteader

Description:

Do you want to escape the hustle and bustle of city life and experience the simple joys of living off the grid? Join us for an eco-adventure on our homestead, where you'll learn the skills and practices of sustainable living, from growing your food to generating your energy. You'll stay in a cozy yurt powered by solar panels and surrounded by the beauty of nature. Whether you're a nature lover, a homesteading enthusiast, or just looking to disconnect and recharge, this experience is for you.

Highlights:

- Learn about sustainable living practices such as permaculture, solar energy, and rainwater harvesting.

- Stay in a yurt (a nontraditional listing) powered by solar panels and surrounded by nature.

- Help with chores on the homestead, such as feeding the animals, collecting eggs, and harvesting vegetables.

- Cook and eat meals made from fresh, locally-sourced

ingredients.

- Enjoy the peace of off-grid living, away from the distractions of technology and the city.

This experience offers something truly unique and memorable for guests who are interested in sustainability and eco-living. By staying on an off-grid homestead, they will get a first-hand experience of what it's like to live sustainably and connect with nature.

Key Takeaways

- Co-hosting is serving as a primary or secondary host in an Airbnb business. It's an excellent way to still get in on the business if you don't own any property.

- You can convince landlords to let you rent their property for Airbnb by guaranteeing long-term rent and top-notch maintenance.

- Guests are after unique experiences. You can create an unforgettable experience by filling market gaps in your chosen niche.

What Next?

- Find market gaps in your niche that you can quickly fill.

- Create a unique concept for your business based on your niche.

- Find out what it would take to co-host or use a landlord's property as your Airbnb.

Taxes! You can't afford to miss your tax payments. Let's talk about taxes in the next chapter.

CHAPTER 13

Handling Tax Issues

The only things certain in life are death and taxes.

–Benjamin Franklin

Handling taxes as an Airbnb owner can be a complex and confusing task. With the increasing popularity of home-sharing platforms, many people have entered the world of short-term rentals and are now responsible for paying taxes on their rental income.

In this chapter, we will explore the basics of taxes for Airbnb owners, including taxes you may need to pay, how to report your rental income, and how to maximize your deductions. Whether you are a new Airbnb owner or an experienced host, this chapter will provide you with the information and resources you need to handle your taxes with confidence and ease. So, grab a cup of coffee, and let's dive into the world of taxes for Airbnb owners.

Understanding Airbnb Taxes

As an Airbnb owner, you are responsible for paying taxes on the rental income you receive from your property. The exact taxes you need to pay will depend on your location and the specific laws of your jurisdiction. Some of the most common taxes for Airbnb owners include:

- **Income Tax**: Rental income is considered taxable income, and you will need to report it on your tax return. The income tax you will owe will depend on your total taxable income, tax bracket, and deductions.

- **Sales Tax**: Depending on your location, you may need to collect and pay sales tax on your rental income. Sales tax is typically a percentage of the rental price and is charged to the guest.

- **Hotel Tax**: In some locations, Airbnb owners may be required to collect and pay hotel taxes, typically a percentage of the rental price.

- **Property Tax**: As a property owner, you may be charged with paying property taxes on your rental property.

It is important to note that these are only some of the taxes that Airbnb owners may be responsible for paying. It is always best to consult with a tax professional or check with your local tax authorities to understand your specific tax obligations.

Additionally, Airbnb provides tools and resources to help you understand and fulfill your tax obligations, such as the Airbnb host tax center, which includes information on taxes for specific countries, and the Airbnb host earnings summary, which provides a detailed report of your rental income for tax purposes.

How to Report Your Income

The exact process of reporting your Airbnb income will depend on your location and the specific laws of your jurisdiction, but generally, the steps are as follows:

- **Keep records of your rental income**: Keep detailed records of your rental income, including the dates of each booking, the rental amount, and any expenses related to your property.

- **Use the Airbnb host earnings summary**: Airbnb provides a host earnings summary, which is a detailed report of your rental income for tax purposes. This report includes information such as the dates of each booking, the rental amount, and any fees charged by Airbnb.

- **Pay any applicable taxes**: Depending on your location, you may need to pay income tax, sales tax, hotel tax, or other taxes on your rental income. You must check with your local tax authorities to understand your specific tax obligations.

- **Seek professional help**: If you have any questions or concerns about reporting your Airbnb income for tax purposes, it is always best to consult a tax professional. They can help you understand your specific tax obligations and ensure that you are reporting your rental income accurately and in compliance with the law.

It is always best to consult with a tax professional or check with your local tax authorities to understand your specific tax obligations.

Taking Account of Your Airbnb Expenses

As an Airbnb owner, you are responsible for paying taxes on the rental income you receive from your property. The exact taxes you need to pay will depend on your location and the specific laws of your jurisdiction, but some of the most common taxes include income tax, sales tax, hotel tax, and property tax. To fulfill your tax obligations, it's essential to keep detailed records of your rental income and expenses, including the dates of each booking, the rental amount, and any related costs. Airbnb provides tools and resources to help you understand and fulfill your tax obligations, such as the host tax center and earnings summary.

> In terms of expenses, you can deduct certain expenses related to your property from your rental income to reduce the amount of tax you owe.

These expenses may include advertising costs, cleaning and maintenance, utilities, depreciation, and other expenses such as insurance, mortgage interest, and property taxes. To take advantage of these deductions, it's essential to keep detailed records of your expenses, including receipts, invoices, and other documentation. Consult with a tax professional or check with your local tax authorities to understand your specific tax obligations and the rules for taking deductions.

Exploring Recent Tax Law Changes

Some of the recent changes in tax laws affecting Airbnb owners include:

- **Collection of state and local taxes**: In 2019, Airbnb began collecting state and local taxes on behalf of hosts in most states in the U.S. This means that Airbnb automatically collects and pays taxes such as state sales tax, local sales tax, and hotel taxes for hosts.

- **Short-term rental tax laws**: In recent years, several states and municipalities have passed laws explicitly targeting short-term rental taxes. For example, some states require Airbnb hosts to pay a state tax on short-term rentals, while others require hosts to pay a local tax.

- **Simplification of tax laws**: In 2020, the U.S. federal government passed the Remote Workers and Employers Assistance Act, which provides a temporary simplified tax regime for remote workers and employers. This includes provisions for collecting taxes on short-term rentals, making it easier for Airbnb hosts to comply with their tax obligations.

- **Rental income reporting**: Airbnb income is taxable, and owners must report their rental income on their tax returns. This includes the reporting of any expenses related to the property, such as advertising, cleaning, and maintenance.

It's essential to remember that the tax laws for Airbnb in the

U.S. are subject to change and that specific tax laws may vary by state or municipality. It's always best to consult with a tax professional or check with your local tax authorities to understand your specific tax obligations.

IRS Forms

IRS forms are forms used by the U.S. Internal Revenue Service (IRS) to report various types of income and expenses for tax purposes. The forms Airbnb hosts need to use will depend on their tax obligations and the kind of income they are reporting. Some of the most common IRS forms used by Airbnb hosts include:

- **Form 1040**: This is the standard individual tax return form used by U.S. taxpayers to report their taxable income to the IRS. Airbnb hosts need to report their rental income on this form.

- **Schedule E (Form 1040)**: This form reports rental income and expenses related to rental properties, including short-term rentals like those listed on Airbnb. Airbnb hosts will use Schedule E to report their rental income and deductible expenses related to their property.

- **Form W-9**: This form is used by U.S. taxpayers to provide their taxpayer identification number (TIN) and other information to entities that pay them. Airbnb hosts may need to give Airbnb this form to receive payments for their rentals.

- **Form 1099-K**: This form reports third-party network transactions. If an Airbnb host receives over $20,000 in gross payments and more than 200 transactions through Airbnb, they may receive a Form 1099-K from Airbnb.

- **Form 1099-MISC**: This form reports miscellaneous income to the IRS. Airbnb hosts may receive a Form 1099-MISC from Airbnb if they receive rental income through the platform.

It's essential to remember that these are general guidelines and that specific tax obligations and requirements may vary depending on the host's location and circumstances. It's always best to consult with a tax professional or check with your local tax authorities to understand your specific tax obligations and ensure that you are using the correct forms.

The 14-Day Grace Period

The 14-day grace period is a policy used by Airbnb that allows hosts to cancel a reservation up to 14 days before the check-in date without penalty. This policy was introduced to provide hosts with some flexibility in managing their listings and to accommodate last-minute changes in their plans or circumstances.

The 14-day grace period applies to reservations made through the Airbnb platform. It typically covers cancellations made for any reason, including host availability changes, unexpected events, and other circumstances. Hosts are not required to provide a basis for canceling a reservation during the grace period, and they will not be charged a cancellation fee.

It's essential to keep in mind that the 14-day grace period may not apply in all circumstances and that the specific terms of the policy may vary depending on the location, type of listing, and other factors. Hosts should review the cancellation policy for their specific listings and consult with Airbnb customer support if they have any questions or concerns.

Occupancy Taxes

The purpose of these taxes is to generate revenue from tourists visiting the area. Many jurisdictions have imposed or are considering imposing occupancy taxes on short-term rentals, including Airbnb. These taxes are similar to hotel taxes and are typically calculated based on the rental amount and the length of stay (Schneider & Davidoff, 2017).

The amount of the tax varies depending on the location, and the type of accommodation, and the funds generated are typically used to support local tourism initiatives, cultural events, and infrastructure improvements.

Occupancy taxes are typically paid by the guests who are staying in the accommodations, and they are usually added to the nightly room rate. Some cities also impose similar taxes on vacation rentals, such as those rented through platforms like Airbnb. In some cases, these taxes may be subject to change, so it is always a good idea to check the local regulations before making a reservation.

Maximize Your Airbnb Revenue

By following these tips, you can increase your profit potential and make your Airbnb hosting experience more successful. Make sure your listing is appealing, with high-quality photos and a well-written description. Providing extra amenities, such as toiletries and snacks, can help differentiate your listing and earn positive reviews from guests.

Key Takeaways

- As an Airbnb owner, you are responsible for paying taxes on the rental income you receive from your property.

- Airbnb provides tools and resources to help you understand and fulfill your tax obligations.

- The 14-day grace period is a policy used by Airbnb that allows hosts to cancel a reservation up to 14 days before the check-in date without penalty.

What Next?

Did you take any notes? Compare them with a friend who has also read this book. Don't forget to implement all the instructions listed in this book.

Conclusion

Starting and running a successful Airbnb business can be fulfilling and profitable. However, it requires meticulous planning and a thorough understanding of the Airbnb platform and its features. The information contained in this book provides a comprehensive guide to help you navigate the Airbnb ecosystem and build a thriving Airbnb business.

First, it's essential to understand the Airbnb business model and how it differs from traditional hotel or bed-and-breakfast establishments. Airbnb is a unique platform that connects hosts with guests and provides a wide range of amenities, including online booking and payment systems, a robust user review system, and an insurance policy that protects hosts and guests. By leveraging these features, hosts can create a welcoming and comfortable environment for guests while earning a steady income.

Finding your niche is critical for success in the Airbnb market. Your niche could be anything from offering a unique property in a popular tourist destination to catering to a specific group of travelers, such as families or pet owners. By identifying your niche, you can differentiate your property and attract the right guests.

Location is another crucial factor that can impact the success of your Airbnb business. Consider the proximity of your property to popular tourist attractions, transportation, shopping, and dining options; additionally, research local laws and regulations, as well as the competition in the area.

Next, the type of property you offer is also crucial. This could be a single room in your home, a standalone unit, or even an entire house. Whatever type of property you choose, ensure it is well-maintained and has all the amenities and comforts for guests. This includes a comfortable bed, fast Wi-Fi, and essential household items like linens and toiletries.

One of the keys to success in the Airbnb business is having a well-designed and well-maintained property. This means that you should take the time to research and choose the right location for your property, select appropriate furnishings and amenities, and create an appealing and functional living space for your guests. To help with this process, it is recommended that you use high-quality photos and descriptions to showcase your property and make sure to respond promptly to any inquiries or requests from guests.

Another crucial aspect of running a successful Airbnb business is to provide excellent customer service to your guests. This means that you should be available to answer questions and provide support throughout their stay, and you should also be proactive in addressing any issues that may arise. You can also enhance the guest experience by providing information on local attractions, restaurants, and transportation options and being responsive to special requests or needs.

> Providing a great guest experience will not only help you attract more bookings but will also lead to positive reviews and word-of-mouth recommendations.

This, in turn, will help you build a strong reputation in the Airbnb community and further increase your rental's visibility and popularity. A unique guest experience is the ultimate key to success in the Airbnb business. This includes a clean and comfortable space, excellent communication, and a willingness to go above and beyond to ensure your guests have a memorable stay. For example, you can provide local recommendations, offer additional amenities like breakfast or transportation, or even add special touches like fresh flowers or a personalized welcome note.

Additionally, it's important to consider the legal and regulatory requirements of running an Airbnb business. This includes obtaining the necessary licenses, permits, and insurance, as well as following local zoning and safety regulations. It is also important to be aware of the Airbnb host policies, including the Airbnb cancellation policy, which govern the relationship between hosts and guests. By understanding these requirements, you can avoid potential legal issues and maintain good relationships with your guests.

Taxes are also an important aspect to consider when starting and running a successful Airbnb business. Depending on where your property is located, you may be required to collect and remit taxes, such as hotel taxes, occupancy taxes, and state taxes. Consult with a tax professional to ensure you comply with all local laws and regulations.

Co-hosting is a valuable strategy for managing your Airbnb business, especially if you have multiple properties or need time off from hosting. A co-host can handle the day-to-day operations of your business, from managing reservations to cleaning and maintenance. Make sure to choose a co-host you trust and have open communication with to ensure the success of your Airbnb business.

It's important to continually evaluate and adjust your Airbnb business strategy to ensure that you are staying ahead of the competition and meeting the changing needs and expectations of your guests. This includes monitoring your property's performance, gathering feedback from guests, and making changes or improvements as needed. Additionally, it's wise to stay informed about industry trends and best practices and to take advantage of any new features or tools that Airbnb may offer to help you grow and improve your business.

In conclusion, starting and running a successful Airbnb business is rewarding and challenging. Following the best practices and tips outlined in this book, you can build a thriving Airbnb business and provide guests with a comfortable and enjoyable experience. Whether you're just starting or looking to take your Airbnb business to the next level, this guide will help you achieve your goals and succeed in this exciting and dynamic market.

Reasons Why You Should Start an Airbnb Business

Starting an Airbnb business can be a highly lucrative and

fulfilling venture for those who are willing to put in the effort to make it succeed. Here are some reasons why you should consider starting an Airbnb business:

- **Flexibility**: You can operate your Airbnb business on your terms and schedule. Whether you want to rent a room in your home or an entire property, you can choose how much or how little you want to do.

- **Low start-up costs**: Compared to starting a traditional brick-and-mortar business, starting an Airbnb business can be relatively inexpensive. You likely already have many of the basic supplies needed, such as bedding and towels, and you can invest in additional furnishings and equipment as you grow.

- **High potential for earnings**: Depending on your location, you can earn a substantial amount of money by renting out your property on Airbnb. With proper marketing and attention to detail, you can attract a steady stream of guests and generate a substantial passive income.

- **Opportunity for networking**: By hosting guests worldwide, you can build connections and relationships with people from diverse backgrounds and cultures. This can be a great way to expand your personal and professional network.

- **Potential for growth**: If your Airbnb business succeeds, you may expand and rent out additional properties. This can give you even more opportunities to earn a passive income and grow your business.

In conclusion, starting an Airbnb business can significantly supplement your income and potentially build a successful, flexible company. With low start-up costs and the potential for high earnings, it's worth considering as a side hustle or full-time venture. Just be sure to research, follow all local regulations, and provide a clean and comfortable space for your guests.

Bonus Chapter!

10 Tips to Become Financially Free

1. **Set clear and specific financial goals**: Determine how much money you want to earn and what you want to use it for, such as paying off debt, saving for retirement, or building an emergency fund.

2. **Make a budget**: Make a realistic budget that accounts for your monthly expenses and savings goals, and stick to it.

3. **Invest in yourself**: Consider taking courses or obtaining certifications that can help you improve your skills and increase your earning potential.

4. **Network:** Build professional relationships and network with others in your field.

5. **Be proactive**: Seek out new job opportunities, freelance projects, or other sources of income. Don't wait for opportunities; actively look for them.

6. **Diversify your income streams**: Consider multiple sources of income, such as a side business, investments, or rental property, to reduce your financial risk and increase your earning potential.

7. **Save and invest**: Make sure to save a portion of your monthly income, and consider investing in various assets, such as stocks, bonds, and real estate.

8. **Manage your finances wisely**: Make intelligent financial decisions and avoid debt as much as possible. Live within your means and avoid overspending.

9. **Continuously improve**: Stay updated on the latest trends and technologies in your field and actively seek out ways to improve and increase your value to employers or clients.

10. **Stay disciplined and focused**: Consistency is vital to earning and achieving financial success. Stay focused on your goals, and maintain discipline and good habits, such as saving regularly, to ensure long-term success.

10 Tips to Improve Your Airbnb

1. **Determine your style**: Decide on the overall style and look you want for your Airbnb space, which will guide your purchasing decisions.

2. **Focus on comfort**: Prioritize comfortable furniture, bedding, and linens for your guests, as this is a crucial factor in their overall enjoyment of the space.

3. **Invest in high-quality items**: Buy durable and well-made items that will last and provide value for years.

Avoid cheap, flimsy items that will need to be replaced frequently.

4. **Consider the space**: Make sure the items you purchase fit the size and layout of your Airbnb rental, and don't overcrowd the space.

5. **Keep it practical**: Choose functional items that serve multiple purposes, such as a coffee table that doubles as storage, and maximize the use of space.

6. **Pay attention to lighting**: Good lighting can have a significant impact on the overall atmosphere of your Airbnb. Consider investing in different types of lighting, such as overhead, table, and floor lamps, to create a warm and inviting ambiance.

7. **Provide amenities**: Consider purchasing items that make your Airbnb stand out, such as a high-end coffee machine or a Blu-ray player, to provide added value for guests.

8. **Focus on the bathroom**: A well-appointed bathroom can be a big selling point for guests. Invest in high-quality towels, shower curtains, and toiletries to make the space feel luxurious.

9. **Add personal touches**: Include personal touches, such as family photos, artwork, or books, to make the space feel more like a home and less like a hotel.

10. **Be open to feedback**: Get guest reviews after their stays to see what they liked and felt was missing. Use

this feedback to make improvements and tailor your purchasing decisions to better meet the needs of your guests.

10 Tips to Welcome Guests

1. **Provide clear and concise instructions**: Make sure guests know how to access your property, where to park, and how to operate appliances and other equipment.

2. **Be responsive**: Respond to guests' inquiries and messages promptly and courteously to ensure they feel valued and appreciated.

3. **Stock the essentials**: Make sure the space is equipped with the essentials, such as clean linens, towels, soap, and toilet paper, to make guests feel comfortable and at home.

4. **Leave a welcome note**: A handwritten note welcoming guests and providing important information, such as Wi-Fi passwords or local recommendations, can help set a positive tone for their stay.

5. **Provide local recommendations**: Leave a list of local restaurants, attractions, and other places of interest to help guests maximize their stay.

6. **Offer amenities**: Consider providing extra amenities, such as a basket of snacks, coffee, or tea, to make guests feel welcome and appreciated.

7. **Make it easy to check-in**: Make check-in as smooth and straightforward as possible by providing clear instructions, having a flexible check-in time, and providing keyless entry options.

8. **Be available**: Make sure guests know how to reach you in case of any issues or questions during their stay.

9. **Pay attention to cleanliness**: Make sure the space is clean and tidy, with fresh linens and towels, to ensure a positive first impression.

10. **Be flexible**: Be open to accommodating guests' needs and requests, such as a late check-out or a special request, to ensure a positive experience. Showing your willingness to go the extra mile can help create a memorable and enjoyable stay for your guests.

10 Tips to Get Positive Feedback

1. **Offer a welcoming atmosphere**: Make sure the space feels warm and inviting, with personal touches and comfortable furnishings.

2. **Respond promptly**: Respond to guests' inquiries and messages promptly and courteously to show them that you value their business and are dedicated to their comfort and satisfaction.

3. **Stock the essentials**: Ensure the space is equipped with the essentials, such as clean linens, towels, soap, and

toilet paper, to ensure guests have everything they need for a comfortable stay.

4. **Provide clear and concise instructions**: Ensure guests have all the information they need to access the property and use appliances and equipment by providing clear and concise instructions.

5. **Pay attention to detail**: Little touches, such as a bowl of fruit or a bottle of wine, can significantly impact the overall guest experience.

6. **Offer flexibility**: Be open to accommodating guests' needs and requests, such as a late check-in or an early check-out, to ensure they have a positive experience.

7. **Solve problems quickly**: If a guest reports a problem, respond promptly and resolve it as soon as possible to prevent it from affecting their stay.

8. **Show your guests around**: Let them have information about the surrounding area. You should also recommend restaurants, activities, and other local attractions they might like.

9. **Follow up with your guests**: Doing so even after their stay will show that you value their opinion and care about their experience.

10. **Show appreciation**: Express gratitude for guests' business by leaving a thank-you note or offering a small gift. Showing that you appreciate their business can help

create a positive and memorable experience for your guests.

10 Tips to Get Focused on Your Service

1. **Set clear goals**: Determine what you want to achieve with your Airbnb rental and set clear, measurable goals to help you stay focused.

2. **Know your target audience**: Understand your guests' needs and preferences so that you can tailor your services and offerings to meet their expectations.

3. **Provide value**: Offer guests value beyond just a place to stay. Unique amenities, personalized recommendations, and added extras make their stay special and memorable.

4. **Communicate effectively**: Respond promptly to guests' inquiries and messages and inform them of any updates or changes that may affect their stay.

5. **Maintain high standards of cleanliness**: Make sure the space is always clean, tidy, and well-maintained to ensure guests have a positive experience.

6. **Offer a personalized touch**: Personalize the space with personal touches, such as a welcome note, a basket of snacks, or a bottle of wine, to make guests feel valued and appreciated.

7. **Stay organized**: Keep track of your guests' bookings, cleaning schedules, and other vital details to ensure a smooth and seamless experience for both you and your guests.

8. **Continuously improve**: Seek feedback from guests and use it to improve your service, amenities, and offerings.

9. **Stay up-to-date**: Keep up with industry trends and best practices to ensure you are offering the latest and greatest in terms of amenities and services.

10. **Prioritize customer service**: Prioritize customer service by promptly responding to guests' needs and concerns. By delivering exceptional service, you can build a positive reputation and attract repeat business.

References

Airbnb reimagines luxury travel with Airbnb luxe. (2019, July 11). Airbnb. https://news.airbnb.com/en-au/airbnb-reimagines-luxury-travel-with-airbnb-luxe/

Aiyden, R. (2019, September 20). *How 3 guys turned renting air mattresses in their apartment into a $31 billion company, Airbnb.* Insider. https://www.google.com/amp/s/www.businessinsider.com/how-airbnb-was-founded-a-visual-history-2016-2%3famp

Ashok. (n.d.). *Warren Buffett Quote.* Learn Stock Market. https://www.learnstockmarket.in/quote/make-money-while-you-sleep-or-work-until-you-die-warren-buffett/#:~:text=The%20world's%20most%20successful%20investor,misunderstand%20this%20quote%20from%20Buffett.

Benjamin Franklin's last great quote and the constitution. (2022, November 13). National Constitution Center. https://www.google.com/amp/s/constitutioncenter.org/amp/blog/benjamin-franklins-last-great-quote-and-the-constitution

Dodds, W, B., Monroe, K. B., & Grewal, D. (1991). Effects of price, brand, and store information on buyers' product evaluations. *Journal of Marketing Research, 28* (3), 307–319. https://doi.org/10.2307/3172866.

Global vacation rental market size. (2022). Statista. www.statista.com/outlook/374/100/vacation-rental/worldwide#market-revenue

Hering, E. L. (2018, November 5). *4 hospitality rules I learned from Danny Meyer.* Global Leadership Network. https://globalleadership.org/articles/leading-organizations/4-hospitality-rules-i-learned-from-danny-meyer/?locale=en

Hospitality quotes: 10 we could all learn from. (2021, June 1). Town Square. https://beambox.com/townsquare/10-inspirational-hospitality-quotes-we-could-all-learn-from

Jang, Y. & Lee, J. (2019). Non-traditional listings in the sharing economy: an exploration of Airbnb's impacts on housing and urban development. *Journal of Urban Affairs, 41*(3), 361–378. https://doi.org/10.1080/07352166.2018.1492437

Johnson, E., & Smith, A. (2019). Exploring the guest search experience in Airbnb: a multi-method study. *Tourism Management, 70,* 1–13. https://doi.org/10.1016/j.tourman.2018.12.005

Johnson, K. (2019, January). The Guest-Centric Approach to Hospitality: A Review of the Literature. *International Journal*

of Hospitality Management, 76,(1), 1–10.
https://doi.org/10.1016/j.ijhm.2018.07.001

Kim, J. & Lee, Y. (2019). The influence of photographic content on Airbnb rentals. *Tourism Management, 68,* 15–27. https://doi.org/10.1016/j.tourman.2018.09.008

Kim, K., & Kim, Y. (2020). Responsible hosting in the sharing economy: an exploratory study of Airbnb hosts. *Journal of Business Research, 118,* 347–357. https://doi.org/10.1016/j.jbusres.2019.12.011

Kim, Y., & J. Lee. The impact of guest satisfaction on hotel profitability: evidence from South Korea. *Tourism Management, 59,* 12–22, https://doi.org/10.1016/j.tourman.2017.06.005.

King, R. A., & Arpen, S. (2020). Estimating investment returns for airbnb properties. *Journal of Tourism and Hospitality Management, 8*(2), 1–15. https://doi.org/10.5296/jthm.v8i2.15075

Li, H., Song, H., & Qi, L. (2018). The role of trust in online marketplaces: the case of Airbnb. *Sustainability, 10(4),* 1239. https://doi.org/10.3390/su10041239

Li, J. & Kwok, K. (2020). The effect of cancellation policies on airbnb rentals. *Journal of Tourism and Hospitality Management, 8*(1), 1–11. https://doi.org/10.5296/jthm.v8i1.15248

Liu, K. & Wang, Y. (2021). The impact of automation on airbnb hosting: evidence from a natural experiment.

Tourism Management, 79, 1–13.
https://doi.org/10.1016/j.tourman.2021.02.011

Marinaki, A. (2022, December 14). *80 glorious marketing quotes to empower and inspire you.* Moosend.
https://moosend.com/blog/marketing-quotes/

My rich dad taught me to focus on passive income and spend my time acquiring the assets that provide passive or long term residual income...passive income from capital gains, dividends, residual income from business, rental income from real estate, and royalties. (n.d.). AZ Quotes.
https://www.azquotes.com/quote/1028625

Nguyen, T. & Tran, N. (2020). Guest-centric planning: an approach to optimizing airbnb listings. *Tourism Management, 71,* 113–123.
https://doi.org/10.1016/j.tourman.2019.09.005

Quotes on pricing. (n.d.). Ebitda Catalyst.
https://www.ebitdacatalyst.com/quotes-on-pricing/

Scarlett, K. (2021, August 5). *Benefits of becoming an airbnb host. great dwellings.*
https://www.greatdwellings.com/post/benefits-of-becoming-an-airbnb-host

Schreiber, L. (2022, April 12). *Short-term rental property investment: 5 ways to increase profit.* Northeast Private Client Group.
https://northeastpcg.com/blog/short-term-rental-property/

Sun, L. (2022, August 12). *Where will Airbnb stock be in 1 year?*. Nasdaq. https://www.nasdaq.com/articles/where-will-airbnb-stock-be-in-1-year

Susanto, W., Indrawan, M., & Soetjipto, S. (2012). The importance of market research in developing a successful business plan. *Journal of Entrepreneurship, 17*(1), 123-130. https://doi.org/10.1177/0971355711424240

The occasional affair quotes. (n.d.). Good Reads. https://www.goodreads.com/work/quotes/26679496-the-occasional-affair-a-practical-plan-for-life-s-everyday-parties

Vacation rentals - worldwide. (n.d.). Statista. https://www.statista.com/outlook/mmo/travel-tourism/vacation-rentals/worldwide#:~:text=Revenue%20in%20the%20Vacation%20Rentals,to%20hit%2011.3%25%20by%202027.

Value quotes. (n.d.). Brainy Quote. https://www.brainyquote.com/topics/value-quotes

What is passive income and how do you create it?. (n.d.). Wonderlust Worker. https://www.wanderlustworker.com/tag/passive-income-ideas/

Zervas, G., Proserpio, D., & Byers, J. (2017). The impact of Airbnb on housing markets: A systematic review of the literature. *Journal of Urban Economics, 98,* 17–31. https://doi.org/10.1016/j.jue.2016.09.003

Zhang, L. & Chen, X. (2021). The impact of co-hosting on airbnb listing performance. *Tourism Management, 78,* 1–11. https://doi.org/10.1016/j.tourman.2020.11.006